POLISH JEWRY
History and Culture

Marian Fuks, Zygmunt Hoffman,
Maurycy Horn and Jerzy Tomaszewski

POLISH JEWRY
History and Culture

Interpress Publishers, Warsaw 1982

Translated by
Bogna Piotrowska and Lech Petrowicz

Designed by
Krzysztof Racinowski

Production editor
Elżbieta Szeszko

Photographs by J. Chodyna, J. Grelowski, M. Kalinowski,
M. Krajewska, J. Morek and T. Prażmowski

Works of art reproduced in this book come from the collections of the Jewish Historical Institute
in Warsaw, the Judaic Museum in Cracow, the Warsaw National Museum and the Museum of
Modern Art in Łódź

This is the two thousand and second book of Interpress Publishers

This book appears also in Polish and German

ISBN 83-223-2002-7

CONTENTS

INTRODUCTION

This is an exceptional and unusual book we are presenting our readers. This is a book about a world which is no more. Though there are among us people who remember this world, it belongs to the past which was destroyed by the Second World War. However this past has not vanished without trace. It has left behind it a wealth of mementoes and treasures of culture.

Polish Jewry. Among the Jews scattered in eighty countries of the world, those from Poland have always held an exceptional position. This is so because it was in Eastern Europe, above all in Poland, that this unique Jewish culture, both sacred and secular, with all its aspects, manifestations and nuances, took shape.

The Second World War dealt a terrible blow to Polish Jewry and its culture. More than three million Polish Jews perished, but much of the centuries-old heritage of Jewish culture was saved. Nazism destroyed many invaluable monuments of Jewish culture, ruined its sacred buildings with their peculiar rich ornaments, burnt books, manuscripts, old prints, masterpieces of sculpture, painting, graphic art, destroyed households with their wealth of objects of everyday use and customs. But it failed to destroy the Jewish past in Poland. This past has been preserved in literature — both prose and poetry, scholarly and religious writings, and annuals of the Jewish press from the 18th century to the end of the Second World War — in plays and books dealing with the theatre, in painting and music.

Polish Jewry! This is the term used by the Jews all over the world to denote a special community which exerted its influence on culture as well as on the mentality and spiritual and material life of Jews all over the world. There are some fifteen million Jews living on the earth. They live on all continents. And it seems that at least half of them are emotionally linked with Polish Jewry.

The life of Jews in Eastern Europe, including Poland, was far from easy. Their different religion, customs, dress and way of life produced prejudice and sometimes anti-Jewish unrest. Often what turned others against them were their sedate, quiet way of life and their skills. However they kept their sincere loyalty towards the country where they had lived for centuries and which they dearly loved, something they proved with their own blood shed in all national liberation struggles.

Following each historical upheaval Jews left Poland. They left it but they still cherished their sentiment and nostalgic longing for everything which has always connected them with this country.

Emigration scattered Polish Jews over all continents. They brought with them the customs and culture of Polish Jewry, which they preserved till their death and passed on to their successors. After all, nearly all classics of Jewish literature are of Polish origin. The past and the climate of Jewish communities in Poland has been handed down to the future generations by the writers of such calibre as Isaac Leib Peretz, Shalom Aleichem, Sholem Asch and tens of other authors, including the winner of the Nobel prize for literature, Isaac Bashevis Singer, born in Radzymin outside Warsaw.

We shall not list here all the outstanding representatives of political and social life, writers, scholars, artists, Nobel prize winners coming from Poland. Many of those well-known Jews and persons of Jewish origin are of East European provenance, usually from the territory of the Kingdom of Poland, Galicia, Great Poland, Pomerania, or else from pre-war Poland.

And then there are also thousands of simple people, Polish Jews, tradesmen, craftsmen, workers, scholars and artists scattered all over the world, who until today manifest their attachment to their country of origin, to Poland. The best proof of this is the existence of some 400 associations of Polish Jews. These associations carry out animated activity. They publish Memorial Books (*Pinkasim*) for which they painstakingly gather various materials, documents, accounts, memoirs, diaries and descriptions, everything which deals with the most obscure past as well as with the pre-war period, the Nazi occupation, the ghettoes and the concentration camps. They also bring out their own journals, for example the *Bialystoker Shtime* in New York.

For those people this book may make both an interesting and nostalgic reading. We also hope that it will find many readers among those to whom the history of Polish Jews is almost lost in the mists of history.

Marian Fuks

JEWS IN POLAND
UNTIL THE END OF THE 18TH CENTURY

Though the earliest records about Jewish settlement in Poland date from the late 11th century, it is generally held that Jews arrived in Poland much earlier. On the other hand, most scholars discard the theory according to which a large number of followers of the Judaic faith came to Poland from the east in around 965 after the fall of the Khazar state.

The first Jews to arrive in Polish territories in the period of formation of the Polish state were merchants who are referred to in source literature as Radhanites. One of them was Ibrahim ibn Jacob, the author of the first extensive account about Poland, who in the summer of 965 or 966 made a trade and diplomatic journey from his native Toledo in Arab-conquered Spain to the Holy Roman Empire and Slavonic countries.

During the period of feudal disintegration, the development of towns and the commodity money relations favoured numerous settlement by Jews in Poland. Nevertheless, the influx of Jews was brought about above all by persecutions in Western Europe, which gained in force during the crusades. The first source reference concerns the arrival in Poland, in 1097 or 1098, of Jews banished from Prague. Jews from Bohemia, as well as those from Germany, settled mostly in Silesia. They usually engaged in trade and agriculture and also owned landed estates. By the mid-14th century they had settled in thirty-five Silesian towns. Jewish settlement in other parts of Poland proceeded at a much slower pace at that time and thus the first mention about Jewish settlers in Płock dates from 1237, about a Jewish community in Kalisz from 1287 and a Żydowska (Jewish) street in Cracow from 1304.

Earlier, Mieszko III, the prince of Great Poland between 1138 and 1202 and the ruler of all Poland in 1173—77 and 1198—1202, employed Jews in his mint as engravers of dies and technical supervisors of all workers. Until 1206, Jewish moneyers worked on commission for other contemporary Polish princes, including Casimir the Just, Boleslaus the Tall and Ladislaus Spindleshanks. From pure silver they struck coins called bracteates, which they emblazoned with inscriptions in Hebrew.

In 1264, one of the successors of Mieszko III in Great Poland, Boleslaus the Pious, granted the Jews a privilege known as the Kalisz statute. According to this statute, which was modelled on similar decrees issued in Austria, Bohemia and Hungary, Jews were exempted from municipal and castellan jurisdiction and were subject only to princely courts. The same statute granted Jews free trade and the right to conduct money-lending operations which were, however, limited only to loans made on security of immovable property. The Kalisz statute, which described the Jews as "slaves of the treasury", ensured protection of persons, protection of property and freedom in conducting religious rites. They were also given the possibility of organizing their internal life on the principle of self-government of individual communities. Similar privileges were granted the Silesian Jews by local princes, Prince Henry Probus of Wrocław in 1273—90, Henry of Głogów in 1274 and 1299, Henry of Legnica in 1290—95 and Bolko of Legnica and Wrocław in 1295.

These favourable privileges which the Polish princes accorded the Jews, stimulated the reaction against the latter by the Catholic clergy. In 1267, following in the footsteps of similar meetings in

Western Europe, the Council of Wrocław resolved on creating special Jewish quarters separate from the Christian parts of cities and on ordering the Jews to wear a special emblem. Jews were moreover banned from holding offices where Christians would be subordinated to them and were forbidden to build more than one prayer-house in one town. These resolutions, however, though they were reiterated during the subsequent councils in Buda in 1279 and Łęczyca in 1285, were not in practice enforced in view of the profits which the Jews' economic activity yielded to the princes.

The turn of the 13th and 14th centuries saw the end of feudal disintegration in Poland. In the reunited kingdom the role of towns and the burghers grew. The rulers, interested in the development of the commodity money economy, encouraged Jewish immigration. The most outstanding of those rulers was Casimir the Great who in 1334, a year after ascending the throne, acknowledged the privilege granted the Jews in Great Poland by Boleslaus the Pious in 1264. As a result Jews were exempted from German law and came under the jurisdiction of the voivodes and, in cases involving rulers was Casimir the Great who in 1334, a year after ascending the throne, acknowledged the Jagiellonian and his successors until the partitions of Poland in the late 18th century, constituted the basic document defining the general legal status of Jews in Poland. In Lithuania a similar role was played by the privileges accorded by Duke Witold (Vytautas) in 1388—89 to three Jewish communities at Troki, Brest-Litovsk and Grodno.

In the 14th and 15th centuries the main occupation of Jews in Poland was local and long-distance trade. Jews performed the role of middlemen in trade between Poland and Hungary, Turkey and the Italian colonies on the Black Sea. They also took part in the Baltic trade and commercial operations in Silesia. Owing to their links with Jewish communities in other countries as well as experience in trade and money-lending operations, Jewish merchants gained the advantage over local merchants, both in European and overseas trade. Following protests lodged by the rich Polish burghers and the clergy, the scope of credit operations conducted by the Jews was seriously curtailed in the early 15th century. In 1423 the statute of Warka forbade Jews the granting of loans against letters of credit or mortgage and limited their operations exclusively to loans made on security of moveable property.

The amassed capital was invested by the Jews in leaseholds. In the 14th and 15th centuries rich Jewish merchants and money-lenders leased the royal mint, salt mines and the collecting of customs and tolls. The most famous of them were Jordan and his son Lewko of Cracow in the 14th century and Jakub Słomkowicz of Luck, Wołczko of Drohobycz, Natko of Lvov, Samson of Żydaczów, Josko of Hrubieszów and Szania of Bełz in the 15th century. For example, Wołczko of Drohobycz, King Ladislaus Jagiello's broker, was the owner of several villages in the Ruthenian voivodship and the sołtys (administrator) of the village of Werbiż. Also Jews from Grodno were in this period owners of villages, manors, meadows, fish ponds and mills. However until the end of the 15th century agriculture as a source of income played only a minor role among Jewish families. More important were crafts for the needs of both their fellow Jews and the Christian population (fur making, tanning, tailoring).

The expansion of the scope of economic activity carried out by the Jews sharpened competition between them and their Christian counterparts. In the 14th century anti-Jewish riots broke out in Silesia which was ruled by the Bohemian-German dynasty of Luxemburg. These reached their climax during the epidemics of the Black Death when, as earlier in Western Europe, Jews were accused of systematically poisoning the wells. In 1349 pogroms took place in many towns in Silesia and some of the refugees from those towns, as well as Jews banished from West European countries, sought shelter from persecution in Poland.

Streams of Jewish immigrants headed east to Poland during the reign of Casimir the Great who encouraged Jewish settlement by extending royal protection to them. First mentions about Jewish settlements in Lvov (1356), Sandomierz (1367), Kazimierz near Cracow (1386) and several other cities date from the second half of the 14th century. In the 15th century Jews appeared in many cities in Great Poland, Little Poland, Kuyavia, Pomerania and Red Ruthenia. In the 1450s Polish towns gave shelter to Jewish refugees from Silesia which was then ruled by the Habsburgs. In 1454 anti-Jewish riots flared up in Wrocław and other Silesian cities. They were inspired by the papal envoy, the Franciscan friar John of Capistrano. Though his main aim was to instigate a popular rebellion against the Hussites, he also carried out a ruthless campaign against the Jews whom he accused of profaning the Christian religion. As a result of Capistrano's endeavours, Jews were banished from Lower Silesia. Shortly after, John of Capistrano, invited to Poland by Zbigniew Oleśnicki, conducted a similar campaign in Cracow and several other cities where, however, anti-Jewish unrest took on a much less acute form. Forty years later, in 1495, Jews were ordered out of the centre of Cracow and allowed to settle in the "Jewish town" of Kazimierz. In the same year, Alexander Jagiellon, following the example of Spanish rulers, banished the Jews from Lithuania. For several years they took shelter in Poland until they were allowed back to the Grand Duchy of Lithuania in 1503.

Towards the end of the Middle Ages Jews lived in 85 towns in Poland and their total number amounted to 18,000 in Poland and 6,000 in Lithuania, which represented merely 0.6 per cent of the total population of the two states.

The 16th and the first half of the 17th century saw increased settlement and a relatively fast rate of natural population growth among both Polish and Lithuanian Jews. The number of immigrants also grew, especially in the 16th century. Among the new arrivals there were not only the Ashkenazim, banished from the countries belonging to the Habsburg monarchy, that is Germany, Bohemia, Hungary and Lower Silesia (in the 1580's the whole of Silesia had only two Jewish communities, in Głogów and Biała), but also the Sephardim who were driven away from Spain and Portugal. Moreover many Sephardic Jews from Italy and Turkey came to Poland of their own free will.

Towards the end of the 16th century the flood of immigration abated and new communities were founded generally as a result of the movement of the population from the crowded districts to new quarters. In around 1648 Jews lived in over half of all cities in the Commonwealth, but the centre of Jewish life moved from the western and central parts of Poland to eastern voivodships where two out of three townships had Jewish communities. Beginning in the mid-16th century Jews started to settle in the countryside in larger numbers. In the mid-17th century there were 500,000 Jews living in Poland, which meant some five per cent of the total population of Poland and the Grand Duchy of Lithuania.

The legal position of the Jews was still regulated by royal and princely privileges and Seym statutes, with the difference that in 1539 in Poland Jews from private towns and villages became subordinated to the judiciary and administration of the owners. From that time on, next to generally binding privileges, an important role was played by privileges granted by individual lords. On top of that, the legal status of Jews was still influenced by synodal resolutions and the common law. All this amounted to a considerable differentiation in the legal position of the Jewish population. In some cities Jews were granted municipal citizenship, without, however, the right to apply for municipal positions. In many towns, especially the gentry towns, Jews were given complete freedom in carrying out trade and crafts, while in others these freedoms as well as the right to settle were restricted. Finally there were also towns where Jews were not allowed to settle. In the 16th century more than twenty towns obtained the *privilegia de non tolerandis Judaeis*. These included Międzyrzec in 1520, Warsaw in 1525, Sambor in 1542, Gródek in 1550, Vilna in 1551, Bydgoszcz in 1556, Stryj in 1567, Biecz, Krosno and Tarnogród in 1569, Pilzno in 1577, Drohobycz in 1578, Mikołajów in 1596, Chęciny in 1597. In practice, however, this ban was consistently observed only in some of the above mentioned towns. In others, either separate suburbs, the so-called Jewish towns, were formed (for example in Lublin, Piotrków, Bydgoszcz, Drohobycz and Sambor) or the Jews won for themselves the revocation of those discriminatory regulations, for example in Stryj and Tarnogród. The restrictions imposed on the territorial expansion of Jewish quarters forced the Jews to seek the so-called *privilegia de non tolerandis christianis*, or bans on Christian settlement in Jewish quarters. Such privileges were won by the Jewish town of Kazimierz in 1568, the Poznań community in 1633 and all Lithuanian communities in 1645.

Between 1501 and 1648 Jews intensified further their economic activity. This was accompanied by a basic change in the occupational structure of the Jewish population in comparison with the previous period. The primary sources of income for Jewish families were crafts and local trade. The magnates for whom Jewish traders and craftsmen were an important element in their rivalry with the royal towns, generally favoured the development of Jewish crafts. On the other hand, in larger royal towns as well as in the ecclesiastical towns Jewish craftsmen and also Christian craftsmen who were not members of a guild (known as *partacze* or patchers) were exposed to permanent harassment from the municipal authorities and the Christian guilds. They could carry out their occupations only clandestinely. In a small number of towns, for example in Grodno, Lvov, Luck and Przemyśl, some Jewish craftsmen managed to wrest for themselves the right to perform their trade from the local guilds, but that only after having to pay heavy charges.

Despite these difficulties Jewish crafts, which were encouraged by royal starosts and owners of gentry jurisdictions, not only maintained their state of ownership but expanded it considerably. In the mid-17th century Polish and Lithuanian Jews practised over 50 trades (43 in Red Ruthenia) and were represented in all branches of craftsmanship. The most numerous of them were those who made food, leather and textile products, clothing, objects of gold and pewter and glass manufacturers. In the first half of the 17th century Jewish craftsmen founded their own guilds in Cracow, Lvov and Przemyśl. In Biała Cerkiew several Jewish craftsmen (tailors and slaughterers) belonged to Christian guilds in 1641.

In the 16th and the first half of the 17th century Jews played an outstanding role in Poland's foreign trade. They contributed to the expansion of contacts with both the east and the west and were instrumental in importing foreign commercial experience to Poland. Particularly animated trade contacts were maintained by Jewish merchants with England and the Netherlands through Gdańsk, and Hungary and Turkey through Lvov and Cracow. Jews exported not only Polish agricultural produce and cattle but also ready-made products, particularly furs and clothing. In return they brought in goods from east and west which were much sought after in Poland. Jewish wholesalers appeared at large fairs in Venice, Florence, Leipzig, Hamburg, Frankfurt on Main, Wrocław and Gdańsk. In order to expand their trade contacts they entered into partnerships. For example in the mid-16th century Jewish merchants from Brest Litovsk, Tykocin, Grodno and Śledzew founded a company for trade with Gdańsk, while in 1616 a similar company was established by merchants from Lvov, Lublin, Cracow and Poznań. At the turn of the 16th and 17th centuries, in many towns Jewish and Christian merchants set up joint *ad hoc* companies in order to conclude profitable financial operations. In European and overseas trade only a relatively small number of Jews were engaged. The most numerous group among Jewish merchants were owners of shops as well as stall keepers and vendors whose whole property was what they put on show on the stall in front of their houses or on a cart, or what they carried in a sack on their backs.

The expansion of Jewish trade troubled the burghers for whom Jewish competition was all the more painful since they now had yet another rival in the developing gentry trade. The struggle of part of the burghers against Jewish merchants manifested itself among other things in attempts at curtailing Jewish trade. The monarchs, though generally favourably disposed towards the Jews, under the pressure from the burghers and the clergy passed a number of decrees which restricted Jewish wholesale trade to some commodities or else to certain quotas of purchases they were allowed to make. More severe restrictions were contained in agreements concluded between municipal authorities and Jewish communities, though these were seldom observed in practice. In private towns, Jewish trade, which yielded considerable profit to the owners, could develop without any obstacles.

The Jews' trading activity also encompassed credit operations. The richest Jewish merchants were often at the same time financiers. The most famous Jewish bankers were the Fiszels in Cracow and the Nachmanowiczs in Lvov as well as Mendel Izakowicz and Izak Brodawka in Lithuania. Those and a number of other Jews pioneered centralized credit operations in Poland. Though banking institutions created by them mainly financed large Jewish tenancies and wholesale trade, as a sideline they also lent money to the gentry on pledge of incoming crops and to Jewish entrepreneurs. A positive role was also played by much smaller loans granted by Jews to many small craft and trade shops. In many cases these loans were instrumental in opening a business. However, the other side of the matter must not be overlooked. The lending of money at high interest led to the impoverishment of both Jewish and Christian debtors. Some of them were put in prison as a result and their families were left with no means of subsistence. This money lending activity aggravated prejudice against Jews among the burghers, something which had always been there anyway due to their religious and traditional separateness.

An important field of the Jews' economic activity were tenancies. In the period under discussion, next to rich merchants and bankers who held in lease large economic enterprises and the collecting of incomes from customs and taxes, there appeared a numerous group of small lease holders of mills, breweries and inns. There also increased the number of Jewish sub-tenants, scribes and tax collectors employed by rich holders. Some of the latter sometimes attained important positions. For example, in 1525, during the ceremonies connected with the Prussian Homage, without relinquishing his Jewish faith the main collector of Jewish taxes in Lithuania, Michał Ezofowicz was knighted and given the crest of Leliwa. His brother Abraham Ezofowicz, who had been baptised, was also knighted and granted the starosty of Minsk and the office of Lithuanian deputy treasurer.

In the first quarter of the 16th century, Jewish lease holders performed their functions as full-fledged heads of enterprises subordinated to them, for example salt mines and customs offices. "In this period," wrote in 1521 Justus Ludwik Decius, the chronicler of Sigismund the Old, "Jews are gaining in importance; there is hardly any toll or tax for which they would not be responsible or at least to which they would not aspire. Christians are generally subordinate to the Jews. Among the rich and noble families of the Commonwealth you will not find one who would not favour the Jews on their estates and give them power over Christians."

The gentry, who in the 16th century conducted an unrelentless struggle against the magnates, came out against the leasing of salt mines, customs and tolls to the Jews by the lords and the king. Under the influence of the gentry, the diet of Piotrków in 1538 forbade Jews to take in lease public incomes. This ban was reiterated several times by subsequent diets but it proved only partly effective. In 1581 the autonomous representation of the Jews (the Diet of the Four Lands), which gathered in Lublin, took a decision which, under penalty of anathema, forbade fellow Jews taking the lease of salt mines, mints, taxes on the sale of liquor and customs and tolls in Great Poland, Little Poland and Mazovia. This ban was justified in the following way: "People fired by the greed of great income and wealth owing to those large tenancies, may bring unto the whole [Jewish population] — God forbid — a great danger." From that time on, Jewish lease holders were active only in Red Ruthenia, Podolya, Volhynia, west-bank Ukraine and Lithuania. In the tenancies supervised by the Jews as well as in the estates run by the gentry, feudal exploitation of the peasant serfs often led to local revolts which in the Ukraine turned into a Cossack and peasant uprising. The cooperation of the Jewish lease holders with the magnates in the latter's colonial policy caused these revolts often to be held under the slogan of struggle against the Poles and Jews.

Next to crafts, trade, banking and leasing operations, agriculture had become an increasingly important source of income for the Jewish population in the eastern regions of the Commonwealth. Maciej Miechowita, author of the *Polish Chronicle* (1519), when mentioning Jews, says that in Ruthenia they were engaged not only in money-lending and trade but also soil cultivation. In towns Jews owned fields and gardens. In Chełm in 1636 Jewish landless peasants were forced to do serf labour. In villages Jews also toiled the land adjoining the inns, mills and breweries they held in lease.

Some Jews earned their living as paid kahal officials, musicians, horse drivers, factors on gentry estates and in the houses of rich merchants, as middlemen known as barishniki, servants, salesmen, etc. There was also a large group of beggars and cripples without any means of subsistence. Only some of them obtained from time to time assistance from charity organizations and were given a place to sleep in an almshouse. In view of the growing financial differentiation among the Jews social conflicts intensified. The mid-16th century saw the beginning of opposition by Jewish craftsmen against individuals who placed their capital in leather, textile and clothing manufacture. The struggle of the populace against rich merchants and bankers was reflected in the activity of Salomon Efraim of Łęczyca, an outstanding plebeian preacher of the turn of the 16th and 17th centuries. In his book *Ir Gibborim* (The Town of Heroes), published in 1580 in Basle, he sharply criticized the exploitation of the poor by the rich. He also attacked the rabbis who tried to gain the favour of the wealthy Jews. He presented his views not only in his books and lectures in the synagogue, but also during fairs which were attended by numerous Jews.

There are records of joint revolts by Jewish craftsmen and Christian "patcher" against the guild elders. There were also joint revolts of the Jews and the burghers against the gentry. This found expression in an agreement which in 1589 Jews in Kamionka Strumiłowa concluded with the municipal authorities "with the consent of all the populace". The councillors "accepted the Jews into their own laws and freedoms while they [the Jews] undertook to carry the same burdens as the burghers". Jews pledged themselves to help in keeping order and cleanliness in the town, hold guard and take part in anti-flood operations together with Christians. The latter promised that they would "defend those Jews as our real neighbours from intrusions and violence of both the gentry and soldiers. They would defend them and prevent all harm done to them... since they are our neighbours."

The rapid development of Jewish settlement and economic activity was accompanied by expansion of their self-government organization. In the 16th century its structure had no equal in all of Europe. As in the Middle Ages, every autonomous Jewish community was governed by its kahal or a collegiate body composed of elders elected as a rule from among the local wealthies. The kahal organized funerals and administered cemeteries, schools, baths, slaughterhouses and the sale of kosher meat. In the closed "Jewish cities" it also took care of cleanliness and order in the Jewish quarter and the security of its inhabitants. To this should be added the administering of charities such as the organization of hospitals and other welfare institutions and the dowering of poor brides. Another important function was to establish the amount of taxes each individual household in the given community was to pay.

The further hierarchic development of the Jewish autonomous institutions was connected with the difficulties which in the early 16th century the authorities encountered in exacting taxes. Between 1518 and 1522 Sigismund Augustus decreed the foundation of four Jewish regions called lands. Each of these lands was to elect at a special diet its elders, tax assessors and tax collectors. In 1530 the king established a permanent arbitration tribunal based in Lublin which was to examine disputes between Jews from various lands. In 1579 Stephen Báthory called into being a central representation of Jews from Poland and Lithuania with responsibility for exacting poll-taxes which had been introduced for the Jewish population in 1549. This institution, known as the Diet of the Four Lands (*Va'ad Arba Arazot*), was constituted at a congress in Lublin in 1581. The Diet of the Four Lands, which usually was summoned once a year, elected from among its number a council, known as the Jewish Generality. The latter was headed by a Marshal General and included a Rabbi General, Scribe General and Treasurers General. The diets were attended by representatives of both Poland and Lithuania until 1623 when, following the establishment of a separate taxation tribunal for Lithuanian Jews, a separate diet of Lithuanian Jews was also set up. These institutions continued in existence until 1764. The diet of Polish Jews usually convened in Lublin, sometimes in Jarosław or Tyszowce, while the Lithuanian diets debated most often in Brest Litovsk.

The diet or *Va'ad* represented all the Jews. It carried out negotiations with central and local authorities through its liaison officers (*shtadlans*) who, by their contacts with deputies, tried to influence the decisions concerning Jews taken by the Seym and local diets of the gentry. During the sessions of the *va'ads* not only fiscal matters were discussed but also those related to the well-being and cultural life of the Jewish population in the Commonwealth. They took decisions on the lease of state products, the amount of interests in credit transactions among Jews, the protection of creditors against dishonest bankrupts, the up-bringing of young people, the protection of the family, etc.

The *Va'ad* also took decisions on the taxation of the Jewish population, for example for defensive needs of the country. The main tax was the poll-tax. In addition the Jews, like the rest of the burghers, paid taxes for the city's defences. Besides taxes, all townsfolk, irrespective of religion, were obliged to perform certain tasks and contribute money in order to build and expand defensive systems and maintain permanent crews of guards. The Jews, like the Christian population, had personally to contribute to the town's defence preparedness. In the Jewish quarter the most important structure was the fortified synagogue. In the 16th and 17th centuries several dozen such buildings were erected in Poland's eastern borderlands, including such places as Brody, Buczacz, Czortków, Husiatyń, Jarosław, Leszniów, Lublin, Luck, Podkamień, Pomorzany, Sokal, Stryj, Szarogród, Szczebrzeszyn, Szydłów, Tarnopol, Zamość and Żółkiew.

One of the main duties of all townsfolk, including the Jews, was to defend the city as a fortified point of resistance in case enemy troops succeeded in forcing their way through into the country. In the early 16th century in the Grand Duchy of Lithuania to this was added the duty of providing a contingent of soldiers. After 1571 this duty was changed to appropriate money dues. For the first time Jews were ordered to provide an army contingent in 1514 but this obligation began to be exacted more consistently only after 1648. As was the case with the remaining population Jews acquired their military training during obligatory exercises and their fighting preparedness and ability to wield arms were tested during special parades.

The first mention of a Jew's direct participation in battle against enemies of the Commonwealth dates from the mid-16th century. During the reign of Stephen Báthory there served in the Polish army one Mendel Izakowicz from Kazimierz near Cracow. He was a bridge builder and military engineer and during the war against Muscovy rendered considerable services to the Polish army. During the war with Muscovy in 1610—12 in one regiment only, probably one of those belonging to Lisowski's light cavalry, more than ten Jews served at one time. A certain number of Jews also fought on the Polish side in the so-called Smolensk war of 1632—34 and some of them were taken prisoner by the enemy.

The year 1648, when the Cossack uprising under Bohdan Chmielnicki broke up, was a break-through in the history of both the Commonwealth and Polish Jewry. The country was plunged into economic crisis made worse by war devastation. The wars against the Ukraine, Russia, Sweden, Turkey and the Tartars, which Poland fought almost uninterruptedly between 1648 and 1717, brought in their wake a permanent downfall of towns and agriculture and decimated the population. During Bohdan Chmielnicki's revolt and wars against the Ukraine and Russia Jewish communities in the areas occupied by enemy troops were completely wiped out. Some Jews were murdered, some emigrated to central Poland and the rest left for Western Europe. The drop in the number of the Jewish population during the Ukrainian uprisings (1648—54) is estimated as amounting to some 20 to 25 per cent, that is between 100,000 and 125,000. A rapid growth in the number of the Jewish population was recorded only in the 18th century, after 1717. It is estimated that in 1766, when the census of Jews obliged to pay poll-taxes was concluded, there were in the Commonwealth as a whole some 750,000 Jews, which constituted seven per cent of the total population of Poland and the Grand Duchy of Lithuania. According to Rafał Mahler, at this time some 29 per cent of all Jews lived in ethnically Polish areas, 44 per cent in Lithuania and Byelorussia and 27 per cent in regions with a predominantly Ukrainian population. Two thirds of all Jews lived in towns and the remainder in the countryside.

Following the first partition of Poland some 150,000 Jews found themselves under Austrian occupation, about 25,000 in the Russian zone and only 5,000 in Prussia. The population census conducted in Poland in 1790—91 demonstrated a further increase in the number of Jewish inhabitants. Tadeusz Czacki estimated them at over 900,000, that is some 10 per cent of the total population of the then Commonwealth. In the same period (1780) in the Austrian zone there were over 150,000 Jews and several tens of thousands in the remaining partition zones.

The reconstruction of towns after each war took a long time. The quickest to emerge from ruin were the estates of magnates who willingly employed the Jewish population. In the eastern part of the Commonwealth and partly in central Poland Jews played an important role in reactivating crafts, and not only such traditionally Jewish branches as goldsmithery, pewter, haberdashery and glass manufacture, furriery and tailoring, but also tin and copper working, arms production, carpentry, printing, dying and soap manufacture. There appeared in this period a large number of Jewish craftsmen who travelled from village to village, from manor to manor, in search of temporary employment. The material situation of Jewish craftsmen was generally difficult. The pauperization of towns and villages made it hard to sell their products both for Jewish craftsmen and their Christian counterparts. In the large cities, rivalry between the guilds on the one hand and the Jewish and Christian "patchers" on the other bred conflicts. These often ended in compromise and Jews more often than ever before were admitted to Christian guilds. At the same time, next to the old ones, new, purely Jewish guilds were formed, for example in Poznań, Cracow, Lvov, Przemyśl, Kępno, Leszno, Luck, Berdyczów, Minsk, Tykocin and Białystok.

During the wars of the mid-17th century Jewish wholesale trade, both long-distance and foreign, came nearly to a standstill. Only in some cities, for example Brody and Leszno, Jewish merchants, thanks to considerable support on the part of the magnates, succeeded in renewing contacts with Gdańsk, Wrocław, Królewiec, Frankfurt on Oder and to a lesser degree with England. Thanks to the magnates' assistance local, Jewish trade also began to expand. Most shops in the reconstructed town halls were leased to Jews (for example in Staszów, Siemiatycze, Kock, Siedlce and Białystok). Peddling was also spreading as a result of which trade exchange between town and country, interrupted during the wars, was revived.

After the mid-17th century wars radical changes took place in the organization of credits. Large banking houses disappeared and the kahals, instead of being creditors, turned into debtors. Representatives of the gentry and the clergy increasingly often placed their money in Jewish communities at the same time forcing the latter to take genuine responsibility for the debts of individual Jews. In case a kahal was unable to repay its debts, the gentry had the right to seal and close down its prayer-house, imprison the elders and confiscate goods belonging to merchants. In order to safeguard themselves against the lightheartedness of individual debtors the communities applied the so-called credit *hazakah*, which consisted in the community issuing permissions to its members who wanted to avail themselves of credit. Whether someone was given a loan or not was often decided by a clique consisting of the kahal elders. Part of the capital leased from the gentry and the clergy and augmented by means of interest disappeared into the pockets of the kahal oligarchy, while part of it was turned over to nonproductive purposes, for example to financing defence in ritual murder trials, paying for the lords' protection, etc.

In the first half of the 18th century the gentry and the clergy became anxious of the fate of money located in the Jewish communities and the interests from unpaid debts which were growing in a landslide. When the above mentioned methods failed to produce adequate results, the so-called krupki were applied, that is a consumption taxation, the income from which was destined totally for paying off the debts. Finally in 1764 a decision was taken on abolishing kahal banks altogether and servicing debts by taxing each Jew.

As a result of the general impoverishment of the Jewish population in the second half of the 17th and in the 18th century, differences between the people and the kahal oligarchy deepened, the latter trying to pass the burden of the growing state and kahal taxes onto the shoulders of the poorer classes. In several cities, for example in Cracow, Leszno and Drohobycz, the Jewish poor revolted against the kahal oligarchies. A fierce struggle against the kahals was carried out by Jewish guilds which tried to free themselves from their economic dependence. At the same time, especially in larger royal towns, conflicts fired by economic rivalry broke out between Jews and Christians. The tense atmosphere of this struggle, conducted usually under religious slogans, was conducive to the outbreak of anti-Jewish riots and pogroms, for example in Cracow, Poznań, Lvov, Vilna, Brest Litovsk and several other cities. Particularly menacing were ritual trials organized in the period of religious prejudices. However much more dangerous was the situation in the Ukraine where the Jews returned only in the late 17th century. The role played in the 18th century by Jewish lease holders in the Polish magnates' colonial policy turned the anger of the local populace, as was the case during Bohdan Chmielnicki's uprising, against both the Polish gentry and Jews generally. In 1768, during a peasant rebellion called *koliszczyzna*, which was organized under the slogans of "winning independence" and defence of the Russian Orthodox religion, in Humań and several other Ukrainian cities several thousand gentry and several tens of thousand Jews were murdered.

The events in the Ukraine in 1768 turned the minds of the more enlightened section of Polish society to the problem of carrying out fundamental political reforms and solving both the peasant and the Jewish question. The latter was not only discussed in the last decades of the Commonwealth but practical ways of solving it were sought. Many pamphlets and Seym speeches dealt with this matter. Some were for the further limitation of the Jews' economic activity while others spoke of turning the Jews into subjects of the gentry, as was the case with the peasants. Finally there were also those who demanded the expulsion of Jews from Poland. These views were opposed by an enlightened group of the gentry, led by Tadeusz Czacki and Maciej Topor Butrymowicz. This group demanded the limitation of the authority of the kahals and a change in the occupational structure of Jews through their employment in manufactories and agricultural farms. It was also for the assimilation of the Jews and their inclusion in the burgher estate.

In the 1760s the Jewish question was the subject of Seym debates. In 1764 the Seym passed a resolution on the liquidation of the central and land organization of the Jews. In 1768 it decided that Jews might perform only such occupations which were allowed to them by individual agreements with towns. From the point of view of Jews, this meant full dependence on their all-time rival in the economic field, that is on the burghers. The Seym of 1775 undertook the problem of agrarianization of the Jewish community and passed a resolution granting tax exemptions to those Jews who settled on uncultivated land. The same law forbade rabbis to wed those who had no permanent earnings.

Jewish reforms were also discussed during the Great Seym which elected a special commission for Jewish affairs. However this commission did not manage to submit its findings before 14 April 1791, that is the date when the law on towns was passed, on the basis of which Jews were not included in the burgher estate. Later the Jewish question was dealt with several times; however the Four Year Seym failed to approve any fundamental reforms in this field. The only important concession for the Jews during the debates of the Four Year Seym was contained in the law of the police commission of 24 May 1792 which said that Jews, like all other citizens of the Commonwealth, could avail themselves of the right not to be put in prison without a court verdict.

Though no important law concerning the solving of the Jewish question was approved by the Four Year Seym, the very fact that the matter was discussed was welcomed by part of the Jewish community with appreciation. On the first anniversary of the passing of the Third of May Constitution services of thanksgiving were held in all synagogues and a special hymn was published.

Neither was the difficult Jewish question solved in the Prussian and Austrian partition zones. In the Prussian zone, according to the decree issued by Frederick II, the Jewish population was to be subordinated to the Prussian Jewish ordinance (*General-Judenreglement*) of 17 April 1797. The right to permanent residence in towns was granted only to rich Jews and those engaged in trade. Jews were forbidden to pursue those occupations which were already represented in the guilds. The poor Jews, the so-called *Bettel-Juden*, were ordered by Frederick II to be expelled from the country. The activity of Jewish self-government organizations was limited almost exclusively to religious affairs.

In the Austrian partition zone the attitude towards the Jewish question went through two stages, In the initial period, that is during the reign of Maria Theresa and the first years of rule of Joseph II, the separateness of the Jewish population from the rest of Galician society was retained and, with only slight modifications, Jewish self-government was preserved. The poorest Jews were expelled from the country. The remainder were limited in their right to get married, removed from many sources of income and forced to pay high taxes. In the second half of the reign of Joseph II the Jews were recruited into the army (1788) and then, on the strength of the grand Jewish ordinance of 1789 certain restrictions in relation to the Jewish population were lifted and attempts were made to make them equal with the burghers. Expulsions of the Jewish population from Galicia were discontinued, the separate Jewish judiciary was abolished, Jewish self-governement was restricted. Jews were ordered to wear dress similar to the Christian population and obliged to attend either German or reformed Jewish schools. However the separate Jewish tax was retained and their economic activity in the countryside was restricted. Some of these decrees met with a decided opposition on the part of the Jews and were eventually revoked. In 1792 Leopold II, Joseph II's successor, changed the military duty of the Jews into a money contribution, while the decree ordering the Jews to wear Christian dress was never introduced in practice.

In the second half of the 17th century Jews took an increasingly numerous part in the wars fought by the Commonwealth. During wars against the Cossacks and the Tartars, the Jewish population provided infantry and mounted troops. Some young Jews fought in the open field, for example in the battle of Beresteczko. Jews also fought in defence of besieged cities, for example Tulczyn, Połonne, Lvov and others. During Poland's wars with Sweden (1655—60), Russia (1654—67) and Turkey (1667—99) Jews provided recruits and participated in the city's defence (for example Przemyśl, Vitebsk, Stary Bychów, Mohylew, Lvov and Trembowla), together with the burghers and gentry organized sorties to the enemy's camp (for example at Suraż in 1655, in the vicinity of Podhajce in 1667 and in Przemyśl in 1672). The military engineer Jezue Moszkowicz of Kazimierz near Cracow, who in 1664 served in the Polish army, saved heavy mortars and other weapons from being sunk during the war against Russia.

During the Kościuszko Insurrection and wars against Tsarist Russia in 1794 Jews supported the uprising either in auxiliary services or in arms. For example they took part in the April revolution in Warsaw where many of them perished. After the Russian army was repulsed from Warsaw the idea was born to create a separate military unit composed of Jewish volunteers. This idea was backed by the commander-in-chief of the Insurrection, Tadeusz Kościuszko. "Nothing can convince more the far away nations about the holiness of our cause and the justness of the present revolution," he wrote in a Statement on the Formation of a Regiment of Jews, "than that, though separated from us by their religion and customs, they sacrifice their own lives of their own free will in order to support the uprising." The Jewish regiment under Colonel Berek Joselewicz took part in the fighting during the storming of the Praga district of Warsaw by tsarist troops on 4 November 1794. With the blood shed in this war they documented the loyalty of the Jewish population to the cause of the revolution and the slogans it upheld — equality and fraternity.

JEWISH CULTURE IN POLAND UNTIL THE END OF THE 18TH CENTURY

LANGUAGE AND LITERATURE

In Old Poland Jews used two languages. The language which prevailed in the liturgy, schools and religious and philosophical writings was Hebrew. The colloquial language, at least from the beginning of the 15th century, became Yiddish which, though derived from German vocabulary and syntax, differed from German dialects in its sound, the structure of sentences, the order of words and a considerable number of loanwords (between 10 and 15 per cent) from Hebrew.

In later periods the Jewish vocabulary acquired a strong Slavonic element. The oldest text in Yiddish in German territory dates from 1382, while the oldest notes in this language in Poland have been preserved in court books from 1423—37. From 1485 comes the Jewish text of a contract concluded between Jews and the Cracow burghers.

In the 14th century the Yiddish language was used in Italy and Germany to put down songs of Jewish bards modelled on those of wandering minstrels though adapted to the customs and traditions of the Jewish population. In the early 16th century in western Europe and towards the end of that century in Poland, a number of tales and chansons de geste were published in Yiddish.

This period also saw the emergence of original Jewish literature derived mainly from biblical legends. In 1602 in Basle an extensive collection of such stories was published under the title *Ma'aseh Book* (The Book of Stories).

At the same time Jewish religious writing was developing. Its aim was to spread the knowledge of the Bible among women who knew little Hebrew or none at all. The first book of this kind was the concordance (or a compilation of texts on the same subject) of Anshel of Cracow, which appeared in Cracow in 1534 as the first book in Yiddish published in Poland. Most popular among Jewish women was the book by Jacob b. Isaac Ashkenazi of Janów Lubelski (1550—1628) entitled *Ze'enah u-Re'enah* (Come and See), published in Yiddish in 1622. It contained not only a popular lecture on the Old Testament expanded and embellished with many legends from the Talmud, but also practical advice and many hints on life. The proof of the high level of learning among Jewish women in the 16th century is the work of Rebecca, daughter of Rabbi Meir Tiktiner (of Tykocin). Well versed in religious and philosophical literature she prepared for print in Yiddish an updated handbook of didactic and educational instructions for Jewish women (the book appeared in 1618, after the author's death). Rebecca was also the author of a joyous song of 80 lines which was sung by women in the synagogue during the Feast of the Joy of the Torah (*Simhat Torah*).

The most important role in the writing of Polish Jews until the end of the 18th century was played by the so-called rabbinical literature (halakhic writings) which dealt mainly with the study of the Talmud (Learning) composed of two parts: the Mishnah or a lawbook (*Halakhot*) from all fields of life, collected and codified in circa 200 by Judah ha-Nasi, and the Gemara or a commentary on the Mishnah.

Next to the strictly religious works there were also books on the philosophy of religion, ethics, didactics, and other subjects, which are also included among rabbinical literature. Its abundance and longevity in Poland — from the 15th to the 18th century — is obvious in view of the fact that knowledge of the Talmud was a necessity in life since the Jews in this period strictly observed all rites and rituals and the rabbinical courts pronounced verdicts in cases involving Jews on the basis of talmudic law. In addition, the knowledge of the Talmud was a precondition of attaining higher social status.

The development of rabbinical literature was further promoted by the rapid expansion of printing facilities. The first Hebrew printing houses were founded in Poland in 1534 in Cracow. They were established by the Halicz brothers. Between 1569 and 1626 a large printing press set up by Izaak of Prościejowice operated in Cracow. In the 17th and 18th centuries attractively produced Yiddish and Hebrew books were published also in Lublin, Żółkiew and other cities.

The main method used by authors of rabbinical literature was the so-called *pilpul* (pepper) or apparently correct reasoning. This method had prevailed in theological writings since the time of Rabbi Jacob ben Joseph Pollack of Cracow (1460—1541).

The crowning work in world talmudic literature was the *Shulhan Arukh* (The Prepared Table) by Joseph Qaro, rabbi of Adrianople and later at Safad (1488—1575), which for many centuries was a handy code for internal use and the final say in the field of Jewish law.

The most outstanding representative of rabbinical literature in Poland was Moses Isserles (1520—72), Qaro's contemporary and commentator on his works. By adapting the *Shulhan Arukh* to the needs of the Ashkenazic Jews (Qaro's work showed a certain prejudice in favour of the Sephardic view), Isserles contributed considerably to the popularization of this book in Central and Eastern Europe. He was moreover the rector of the Cracow yeshiva (higher talmudic college) and author of many works on talmudic law, philosophy, kabbalah, astronomy and other branches of learning.

The remaining representatives of rabbinical literature in its greatest period in Poland (1550—1648) included Solomon ben Jehiel Luria (1510—73), who propagated rational methods of interpretation of the Talmud, Mordecai Jaffe (1530—1612), author of the ten-volume *Levushim* (Attires), Joshua ben Alexander ha-Kohen Falk (1550—1614), rector of the yeshiva in Lvov and commentator on the *Shulhan Arukh,* and Yom Tov Lippman Heller (1579—1654), an ardent opponent of the sophistic method of commenting the Talmud and author of a commentary to the Mishnah.

A separate kind of literature connected with rabbinical writings were apologetic and polemical works in which followers of the Mosaic faith defended the truth of the Old Testament in their disputes with the Catholic and Protestant clergy. The most outstanding representative of this direction in 15th century Poland was Yom Tov Lipmann Muelhausen who lived in Cracow in 1400—25. His polemical treatise etitled *Sefer ha-Nizzahon* (Victory), written in Hebrew, in which he declared war not only on Christians and Karaites but also on Jewish scholasticism, has been preserved. This work, rewritten many times, appeared for the first time in Altdorf in 1644.

Another famous Jewish apologist and polemicist in Poland was Jacob of Bełżec who conducted a dispute in defence of the Jewish faith with Marcin Czechowic, a well-known representative of the Polish Socinians. The latter published in 1581 a book entitled *Odpis Jakuba Żyda z Bełżca na dialogi Marcina Czechowica, na który zaś odpowiada Jakubowi Żydowi tenże Marcin Czechowic* (A Reply of Jacob the Jew from Bełżec to Marcin Czechowic's Dialogues to which that Marcin Czechowic replied). The Karaite Isaac b. Abraham Troki (1533—94), author of the extensive polemical work *Hizzuk Emunah* (The Foundation of the Faith), demonstrated contradictions between the text of the New Testament and the Christian teaching about the Holy Trinity as well as the incongruity between the Catholics' ethic principles and their everyday life. The treatise of Isaac of Troki stirred lively discussions in the Christian world in the 17th century and in the following century it became an object of interest of the encyclopaedists, Voltaire included. Public utterances of Jacob of Bełżec and Isaac of Troki are proof of the much more lenient attitude in relation to the adherents of the Mosaic faith in Poland than in many west European countries where such open defence of the Jewish religion was inadmissible in the 16th century.

In the 17th and 18th centuries, during the Counter-Reformation, this kind of literature disappeared, to re-emerge for a short time in 1757—59, in the period of development of Frankism, when the higher Catholic clergy in Lvov and Krzemieniec staged disputes with representatives of Talmudism and Frankism. Fragments of these diputes, in which the Orthodox Jewish wing was represented by Rabbi Hayyin ben Simhah ha-Kohen Rapaport of Lvov, were published by Dov ber Birkenthal of Bolechów, a participant in these events, in his memoirs.

LAY LEARNING

Next to the talmudic writing there appeared in Poland treatises devoted to the various branches of secular learning. Most often they were written by rabbis who in their theoretical treatises referred to the heritage of Moses Maimonides (1135—1204), the most outstanding representative of Jewish Aristotelianism, a scholar who strove to prove in a rational manner the principles of Judaism. The followers of Maimonides in Poland were the above mentioned Rabbis Solomon Luria and Moses Isserles, as well as Abraham b. Shabbetai Horowitz and Jacob ben Samuel Bunim Koppelman and in the 17th century also Mordecai ben Abraham Jaffe, Eliezer Mann and Manoah Handil ben Shemariah. All of them substantiated the need for reconciling the principles of faith with reason based on the knowledge of secular sciences and repeatedly applied this practice when referring in their treatises to the achievements of mathematics, astronomy and medicine. In the 17th century separate works devoted exclusively to mathematics and mechanics were also written in Poland. Their authors were the mathematicians Jehuda ben Abraham and Jacob of Poznań (1st half of the 17th century) and the mechanic and constructor Jezue Moszkowicz of Lublin (2nd half of the 17th century).

The 17th century also saw great development in chronicle writing. The most distinguished chronicler was Natan Nata Hannover of Zasław (died 1683), author of the chronicle *Yeven Mezulah* (Miry Pit) published in Venice in 1653 and dealing mainly with the tragic fate of the Jewish population during the Cossack uprising under Bohdan Chmielnicki.

One of the oldest branches of learning practised by Jews was medicine. In the Middle Ages Jewish doctors, famous for their abilities, were willingly invited to papal and secular courts. They acquired their knowledge and skills in Spain and Portugal (until the end of the 15th century), as well as in Italy (mainly Padua) and Germany and Austria (from the mid-18th century on).

Despite obstacles put up by the Church and opposition on the part of Christian physicians, Jewish doctors were highly sought after in Poland. In larger cities there were whole Jewish families of doctors who served both Jewish and Christian patients throughout decades.

The best of the Jewish doctors were employed by Polish monarchs as court physicians. Jews were court physicians to Casimir the Jagiellon, John Albert (Isachko of Spain), Sigismund the Old and Queen Bona (Isachko of Spain, Samuel ben Meshullam and Moses Fishel), Sigismund Augustus (Solomon Ashkenazi of Udine and Solomon Kalohorra whose family came to Poland from Spain) and John Sobieski (Menahem Simhah Emmanuel de Yonah). Jewish doctors were invited to the courts of Alexander the Jagiellon, Stephen Báthory and Stanislaus Augustus Poniatowski.

Of the Jewish doctors who served at magnate courts of, for example, the Myszkowski, Wodzicki, Lubomirski, Potocki, Radziwiłł and Sułkowski families, the most famous was Joseph Solomon

Delmedigo (1591—1655). Born in Candia, Delmedigo had been a disciple of Gallileo and Kepler. He arrived in Poland in 1616. Until 1620 he worked in Lublin and then moved to the residence of the Radziwiłł family at Nieśwież. During his stay in Poland he wrote one of his most important works, *Sefer Elim*, in which he defended the Copernican theory.

At the turn of the 17th and 18th centuries another doctor became famous in Europe. This was Tobias ben Moses Cohn (1652—1729), born in Metz of the family of emigrants from Poland, the doctor and mathematician Moses Kohen. Tobias became a doctor of medicine at the university of Padua. He later came to Poland where he worked as a physician for a long time. He was the author of a treatise written in Latin and Hebrew on zoology and the medical work *Ma'aseh Tuviyyah* (Tobias' Tales) which was in the style of the epoch, punctuated with items of information on geography, astronomy and cosmography.

The further development of secular learning is connected with the Jewish Enlightenment called Haskalah. Though this movement propagated emancipation and assimilation in the field of culture and customs, it however did not discard tradition and was not against religion. The Haskalah arose in Western Europe and its most prominent representative was Moses Mendelssohn (1729—86), an author and philosopher active in Germany. He believed that thanks to a change of customs and reform in education and learning, Jews could emerge from isolation and win equal rights. Mendelssohn's ideas were readily accepted in Poland where even earlier there appeared scholars who wanted to free themselves from the influence of Orthodox rabbis. Among them were two Jews from Zamość, Israel ben Moses Halevi Zamosc, mathematician and philosopher, Mendelssohn's teacher in Berlin, and Solomon ben Joel Dubno, lawyer, commentator and traslator of the Pentateuch into German. The main promoters of the Haskalah in Poland were the philosopher Solomon Maimon (1754—1800) and the naturalist and mathematician Menahem Mende Lewin of Satanów (1749—1823). Though he lived abroad permanently Solomon Maimon, as a representative of the most progressive popular movement within the Haskalah, prepared, with a thought to Jews in Poland and Lithuania, a cycle of popular science books, mainly in the field of mathemathics and physics. Of his output, the most famous were the works in which he criticized Kant (1792) and an autobiography which is a first-class source on the history of not only Jews but the whole of Polish society in the late 18th century. Maimon maintained that the assimilation and emancipation of Jews, a change in their fortunes, may be promoted in a large measure by enlightened rulers. In his dedication to King Stanislaus Augustus Poniatowski on a copy of his *Versuch über die Transzendentalphilosophie* (An Attempt at Philosophy concerning Aprioristic Methods of Cognition, 1790), he stressed that he would have been very happy had he been able to "contribute to the formation among the honourable Poles of a favourable opinion about my nation... and to convince them that they [the Jews] lack neither talent nor good will, but they have not had a permanent spiritual leadership".

Mendel Lewin of Satanów was active mainly in the period of the Four Year Seym. He supported the so-called Jewish reforms which he tried to put into practice with the help of Polish magnates, for example Prince Adam Czartoryski.

In 1789 Lewin published a treatise in French in which he presented his views on reform of the Jewish question. He demanded that the state should ensure Jews religious tolerance, abolish special taxes for the Jewish population and reorganize the constitution of the rabbinate. The state should try to win the trust of the young people through giving them freedom, accustoming them to obedience and inculcating in them attachment to the country. He drew particular attention to the need for changing the educational system and moulding in young people a critical sense in relation to religious authority. He also stressed the necessity of the Jews learning the Polish language.

All this was to contribute to the gradual elimination of religious fanaticism, prejudice and backwardness among the Jews and to breaking away from the isolation the Jewish population found itself in.

In order to reach the Jewish populace with his ideas he translated many of his works into Yiddish. The same was done by other followers of the Haskalah, known as the Maskilim (the Enlighteners), including Doctor Moses Marcuse, author of a popular work on folk medicine *Sefer Refu'ot* (Drugs), published in Yiddish.

The assimilation processes propagated by the supporters of the Haskalah encompassed only the richer strata. The majority of the Jews from the middle and lower classes continued to adhere to their tradition, culture and customs until the end of the 18th century.

The Enlightenment movements accelerated the development of secular literature, philosophy, mathematics, astronomy and medicine. They also prompted a change in the attitude of some Orthodox representatives, who in the second half of the 18th century formed a group of enlightened talmudists.

Perhaps the most famous of them was Rabbi Elijah ben Solomon Zalman of Vilna (1720—97), called the Vilna Gaon (excellency). He wrote not only commentaries to the Bible and kabbalist books but also works on trigonometry. Knowledge of the exact sciences, especially of mathematics and astronomy, was considered by the Vilna Gaon as one of the most important paths leading to the deepening of religious studies since, as he wrote, "Order and knowledge are closely connected with one another". The work of Elijah of Vilna was continued by his disciple Baruch of Szklov (1740—1812), author of books on astronomy, anatomy and hygiene and translator from English of Euclidean geometry (1780) and an English handbook of trigonometry (1784).

Towards the end of the 18th and at the beginning of the 19th century, many enlightened Polish Jews, mainly those from among the Maskilim, who made a name for themselves in the field of learning, developed lively scientific and political activity in Western Europe. Among them were Aron Polak and Zulkind Hulwicz of Lublin, participants and political leaders of the French Revolution; Juda Litvak, the excellent Dutch mathematician; Israel Lyons, professor of Oriental studies in Cambridge; Hayman Hurwicz, Bible scholar and professor at the University of London; and Isachar ber Falkensohn, author of a volume of poetry published in Germany under the title *Geschichte von einem polnischen Juden* (The History of the Polish Jew). The last of these, having obtained the doctorate in medicine at Halle University in 1772, returned to Poland and opened medical practice in Mohylew.

MYSTICISM, KABBALAH, MESSIANIC MOVEMENTS

Messianic and mystical movements appeared among the Jews in particularly dangerous periods. These ideas were propagated in the period of antiquity by the prophets Isaiah and Ezekiel and their followers, who spoke about the approaching coming of a Messiah who would deliver the Jewish people. In time a special branch of learning of a mystical and apologetic character called kabbalah (tradition) emerged in Jewish philosophy. In the 13th century it developed into a philosophical system based on the neo-Platonic theory of emanation as a reaction to the rationalistic philosophy of Moses Maimonides. Towards the end of the 13th century the Spanish Jew Moses ben Shem Tov de Leon published in Aramaic the *Sefer ha-Zohar* (The Book of Splendour), the most important work of Jewish mysticism which contained a concise elucidation of theoretical Kabbalah. This book was not a subject of learning in Jewish schools, as were the Bible and the Talmud, but as a "secret" science it was passed by the teacher to one — the most able and the best liked — pupil.

In the 16th century the so-called practical Kabbalah developed, its most prominent theoretician being Isaac ben Solomon Luria of Palestine (1534—72), called Ha-Ari (the Sacred Lion). He proclaimed that man's soul can free itself from the power of evil spirits through self-immolation, fasting, penance and redeeming of sins, and that after death the sinful soul wanders about and enters the bodies of other people until it cleanses itself of its sins. He spread among his disciples the conviction about the possibility of the Kabbalists affecting natural and social phenomena by means of the magical power of the biblical text. From among the Polish practical Kabbalists the most influential among the masses was Isaiach ben Abraham ha-Levi Horovitz of Kazimierz near Cracow (1632—89), author of the *Shenei Luhot ha-Berit* (Two Tablets of the Ark of Covenant) in which he propagated the ideas of extreme mysticism and asceticism. According to him the means leading to God are "hairshirt, fasting, ash, tears and mourning". Man should not follow the "whims of his body but the voice of his soul, he should live in trembling and fear, in shame and purity".

The announcement by the adherents of the practical Kabbalah of fasts and recommendation of self-immolation could not soothe the Jewish masses in the period of economic decline, general pauperization of society and ritual trials and anti-Jewish pogroms organized here and there. The Jewish masses wanted sympathy and hope and dreamt about the approaching coming of the Messiah who would free them of all suffering and worry.

In such circumstances there began to spread in Poland a mystical and messianic movement called Shabbateanism.

Contrary to the practical kabbalah, Shabbateanism proclaimed the joy of life and a link with God through ecstasy. The founder of this movement was Shabbetai Zevi (Zvi) who lived between 1626 and 1676. In Smyrna in Asia Minor he announced the approaching coming of the Messiah and the freeing of the Jews of all suffering, owing to which he found numerous adherents in many countries.

In 1660 Shabbetai Zevi, who had proclaimed himself Messiah in the meantime, went with a retinue of thousands of believers to Istanbul to crown himself king of Israel. The Turkish sultan ordered the imprisonment of the false prophet and shortly after the movement of Shabbetai Zevi broke down while he himself, accused of attempting to stir unrest, accepted Islam on the penalty of death. For many long years the conviction prevailed among his followers that their prophet was alive and one day would free the people of Israel from slavery.

In the second half of the 18th century, on a similar background as Shabbateanism, a new movement arose connected with the activity of Jacob Frank (1726—91). Frank was born at Królówka in Bukovina. As a youth he studied Kabbalist books in Multana, Bucharest and Salonica. In 1755 he arrived in Poland and revealed himself as the Messiah, God and successor of Shabbetai Zevi. Like his predecessor he propagated the joy of life and communion with God through ecstasy. Among Polish Jews he found thousands of fanatical adherents since he represented a manifestation of protest against the omnipotence of the rabbis. Soon he was accused of departure from the Jewish religion and of spreading iniquity. Fleeing the persecution of the rabbis, Frank went in 1757 to Wallachia where he became a Muslim. However three years after, having been given permission from the sultan and the Polish king, he returned to Poland where he became a Christian. His God-father was Augustus III. Together with Frank several thousands of his followers were converted to Christianity.

Neither Frankism nor Shabbateanism left any permanent mark on the Jewish religion. The case was different with a much stronger mystical movement called Hasidism (from the word hasidim meaning the righteous, just, devout). The character of this movement was strongly influenced by the protest of the masses against the kahal oligarchy and the learned rabbis. The founder of Hasidism was

Israel ben Eliezer called the Ba'al Shem-Tov (literally the Master of the Holy Name). He was born in Okopy Świętej Trójcy in Podolia in 1700. After years of wandering and taking on various jobs, for example as a beadle in a synagogue, teacher, herbal healer and hermit, in 1736 he appeared as a pious miracle worker. The principles of his teaching were presented in 1780 by his supporter and comrade Rabbi Jacob Joseph of Polonnoye in his commentary to the Pentateuch entitled *Toledot Ya'akov Yosef.*

Hasidism proclaimed that each Jew can be redeemed at any moment, even in the most tragic of circumstances, as long as with the power of his mind he directs the divine sparks in his soul to the Almighty. Communion of thought with God can be achieved not only through common prayer but also by means of individual prayer, while the precondition for its effectiveness is the complete rejection of sadness. The highest degree of piousness is attained by the zaddikim (the righteous ones) who are conceived as an intermediary between man and God. The zaddikim, who were considered by the faithful as perfect people, organized common prayer and joyful feasts with songs and dancing, all in Yiddish, often bordering on ecstasy. Among the Jews, who longed for a bit of joy and a confirmation of their human worth in this gloomy period, Hasidism found more and more adherents despite fierce opposition against this new movement on the part of the followers of the traditional religious forms. As a result of dislike of the kahal oligarchy and talmudists and the fact that the new movement did not break away from the traditional way of life of the people and did not abolish the existing religious prescriptions, Hasidism came out victorious from its struggle with Orthodox talmudism. Towards the end of the 18th century Hasidic teaching encompassed the larger part of the eastern territory of the Commonwealth. In later periods Hasidism opposed the development of secular teaching and educational reform, and, owing to its attempts at preventing Jewish assimilation with Polish society, it became a bastion of backwardness and obscurantism.

ART

Objects of art connected with the religious cult (such as paintings in synagogues, cemetery monuments, illuminated Hebrew manuscripts, sculpted altars and metal ornaments for the scrolls of the Law) were produced almost exclusively by followers of the Mosaic religion, while those objects which were used in everyday life (for example candlesticks, chandeliers, metal trays, tins for crab apples, chalices, jars and cups), were made by both Jews and non-Jews.

Synagogues were generally designed by Jews although the construction itself was usually entrusted to Christian masons.

In the Jewish ornamental arts originating in Poland, motifs from ancient Palestine intermingled with those found in objects produced by artists working for Christian customers. Since the Jewish religion prohibited the showing of human figures, objects of artistic craftsmanship are often decorated with animals which bear symbolic meanings, for example the stag, lion, eagle, tiger, as well as plant motifs such as vine branches, date palms and pomegranates, and seven-branched candlesticks (*menorot*).

The oldest monument of Jewish architecture in Poland is the Old Synagogue in Kazimierz near Cracow, built towards the end of the 14th century and converted in 1570 by Mateusz Gucci. This synagogue was modelled on those in Worms and Regensburg as well as the Altneuschul Synagogue in Prague (early 14th century). The Old Synagogue in Cracow is a two-nave structure with six vaulted fields and two pillars with the bimah in the middle (a raised platform from which the scriptural lesson is read and services conducted) and with the *aron ha-Kodesh* (Ark of the Law) placed on the eastern wall of the synagogue. Alongside two-nave synagogues, one-nave prayer-houses were built in Poland, for example the Old Synagogue in Poznań converted in the 16th century, the synagogue in Gniezno dating from the late 16th century and the Rema Synagogue built between 1533 and 1557 in Kazimierz near Cracow (the name is derived from the abbreviation of names of its founders, Rabbis Moses and Isserles). The 17th century saw the appearance, especially in south-eastern and central Poland, of spacious prayer-houses with four pillars, for example in Łańcut, Rzeszów, Nowogród and Leszno. The architecture of brick synagogues was influenced by secular burgher architecture.

In the eastern borderlands of the Commonwealth which were threatened with constant raids by the Tartars, the kings ordered the construction of fortified prayer-houses which were built either next to the city walls or just outside them. They had thick walls with scarps, battlements, loop-holes and narrow windows placed high up. At the same time timber synagogues were built, their architecture recalling that of manor houses and Catholic churches. Fairly modest when viewed from the outside, inside they demonstrated a magnificent wealth of decoration, especially as regards murals with symbolic motifs. In the Renaissance period, the polychromes of some of the synagogues acquired human figures, for example in the biblical scenes on the walls of the High Synagogue in Cracow. The most sumptuous polychromes were to be found in timber prayer-houses, and among them particularly wealthy as regards form and precision of execution were the multi-coloured paintings in the synagogue in Mohylew. They were painted by Hayyim Isaac Segal of Słuck, whose descendant is Marc Chagall. Rich multi-coloured paintings were also to be seen in the timber prayer-houses in Przedborze, Jabłonów and Kamionka Strumiłowa. Artists modelled their paintings on illuminated Hebrew manuscripts with animal and plant motifs which were created in Poland until the end of the 18th century simultaneously with book graphics. The predominating technique in sculpture was low relief, for example in wooden altar closets and from the 16th century on also in iron and copper wrought doors which closed the altar niches. Magnificent sculptures, which testified to the high artistry of Jewish craftsmen, once decorated the doors of the Rema, High and Old Synagogues in Cracow. An equally high artistic level was represented by sculptures on decorative tomb stones. The most magnificent cemetery monuments were produced in the 17th and 18th centuries in Cracow, Lvov, Lublin, Vilna and Tarnopol. In Warsaw, one of the most beautiful examples of this field of craftsmanship is the tomb stone of the family of Berek Shmulovicz Zbitkover, the work of the outstanding mason and sculptor, David Friendlander.

Until the end of the 18th century in Jewish artistic craftsmanship sacred objects, both those designed for the prayer-houses and those to be used at home during the feasts of the year, predominated. To these belonged the Torah ornaments, Torah crowns and finials (rimmonim), Torah pointers (yadayim), candle holders, silver and gilt plates, bowls and jugs for pouring water on the priests' hands, as well as those used at home, such as chalices, hanukkah lamps, mugs, cups, scent boxes known as balsamniki, censers, tins for crab apples and spice boxes used during the ceremony of circumcision. These objects were often shaped like parrots, fish, acorns, etc. They were decorated with animal and plant motifs by means of various techniques, including moulding, engraving, filigree and granulation, and were often studded with precious stones and decorated with coloured enamels. In the 17th and 18th centuries, next to the traditional symbols and ornaments motifs relating to the general Polish tradition and local predilections appeared. The Polish eagle was emblazoned on parokhets and kapporets, altar sculptures, crowns and lamps, hanukkah candlesticks and synagogue chandeliers. Some kapporets dating from the second half of the 17th century were embroidered with unfurled Polish banners and armour of the Polish army. Much more modest are those objects of Jewish craftsmanship which are not connected directly with the religious cult. To these belong objects produced by goldsmiths, who were fairly numerous in Polish towns, and less numerous engravers and sealers who produced commemorative medals which were in value both in Poland and abroad. Of the Jewish copper engravers active in Poland, particularly famous was Hershel Leibowitz of Nieśwież (1700—70), who produced the painstakingly executed copper-plates which decorated the commemorative book published in honour of the deceased Princess Anne Radziwiłł née Sanguszko as well as 165 copper-plates with likenesses of relatives and ancestors of Prince Michał Radziwiłł.

Jewish embroiderers produced fabrics with gold and silver threads which were used for making altar curtains (parokhets), kapporets and baldachins pitched over the bimah on festive days.

A traditional field of Jewish activity was also bookbinding. Jewish book-binders made leather covers for liturgical books, sometimes studded with precious stones, ivory and mother-of-pearl.

EDUCATION

Education played an important role in the life of Jewish communities. Jews were considered to be people of writing and books. The highest authority was enjoyed not by the rich but by rabbis who were associated with people of wisdom and knowledge. It was an honour for a rich man to have his daughter marry a man, talented though poor, who would devote the rest of his life to the study of the Talmud. For many young people learning became the chief task in life.

Only fragmentary information has been preserved on the system of Jewish education in Poland in the Middle Ages. On the other hand more data is yielded by 16th century sources. At that time it was obligatory to send boys to private or kahal schools. Members of each community paid special taxes for the upkeep of teachers. Between the 16th and 18th centuries a two-tiered system of education existed. The lower level schools were attended by boys aged between four and eight, who learnt to read the Bible, write in Hebrew, translate Hebrew textes into Yiddish, the four rules of arithmetic and the principles of morality and good conduct. The higher level schools, for boys between eight and thirteen years of age, were devoted to the study of the Talmud and its commentaries. Girls from wealthy families obtained their education at home, where, next to Hebrew, they were also taught Yiddish. In all types of school the method used was learning by heart. The education of young people was supervised by special kahal commissions and school fraternities called Hevrat Talmud Torah. In larger cities (for example in Poznań, Lvov, Cracow, Lublin and Przemyśl) special yeshivas or yeshivot were also founded (talmudic academies). They were headed by rabbis called rectors. In the yeshivot a sophistic system of learning prevailed. It consisted in searching for essential and apparent contradictions or *hilluk* (in Hebrew differences) in the Bible and the Talmud and removing them by means of assumptions taken from works of talmudic literature. Use was made here of argumentation based on multiple meanings of words, inconstistencies which were difficult to detect and sophisms. This method was called *pilpul* (pepper) and was critized by some enlightened rabbis.

In the 16th and the early 17th century Polish yeshivot enjoyed high esteem among Jews all over the world. "Nowhere among the Israelites' diaspora was there so much learning as in Poland," wrote Nathan Nata Hannover of Zasław. "Every community had its yeshiva and the wages of rectors were increased more and more in order to let them work with no worry and that teaching could become their profession... Every community maintained its young people and gave them weekly allowances so that they could acquire their knowledge with the rabbi in the yeshiva." This situation, however, changed radically during the wars of the mid-17th century. Many yeshivot were closed down and kahal schools went into decline. A higher level was only maintained by some private schools financed by the wealthy, where as well as the traditional subjects students were taught things which might come in useful in life.

The moralist Hershel Kejdanower complained in 1705 that fathers, instead of sending their sons to kahal schools, where they could be taught Hebrew and the Divine Order, sent them to schools where attention was primarily paid to the study of French and other languages, and the learning of the Order took second place. Kejdanower's remarks concerned only a small group of the nouveaux-riches because in principle Jewish children were brought up according to the traditional patterns. Though it must be said that generally the level of education in Jewish communities in the 18th century was lower than in the 16th and the first half of the 17th century. However with all this, illiteracy among male Jews was an exceptionally rare phenomenon.

During the Haskalah period attempts were made to laicize the Jewish system of education. In the Austrian partition zone the government, striving for the "de-judaization, assimilation and germanization" of the Jewish community, tried by means of drastic methods to introduce a radical educational reform. In 1785 Joseph II issued a decree making it obligatory for Jewish children to attend either general schools or Jewish lay schools. The carrying out of this reform was temporarily entrusted to the Czech Maskil (supporter of the Haskalah or the Jewish Enlightenment), Naphtali Herz Homberg. Over a period of several years, Homberg set up 107 schools for boys and some for girls in which 150 teachers were employed and which were attended by some 4,000 pupils. These schools, where the language of instruction was German, were run in a spirit offensive to the tradition of the Jewish masses and were mistrusted by the parents who declined to send their children to them. In 1806 the schools were finally abolished.

CUSTOMS AND FAMILY LIFE. DRESS

The customs and mores of Polish Jews were shaped in conditions of the growing isolation of the Jewish community from the rest of society, among other things as a result of the conscious policy of both the Church and the Synagogue. In the Middle Ages, when there were not many of them in Poland, they did not differ much in their way of life from their neighbours. This is testified to, for example, by the resolutions of provincial synods in the period between the 13th and 15th centuries, which from time to time had to remind the Catholic population that the latter were not to hold joint feasts with the Jews, to play with them at wedding parties, to dance with them, etc.

In the Kingdom of Poland until the end of the 15th century and in Lithuania even longer, still in the 16th century, Jews did not differ much from their neighbours as regards costume. This can be seen in the preserved stained-glass windows in churches where Jews are shown wearing medieval burgher dress. The same is also corroborated by the so-called second Lithuania statute of 1526 where we read that "Jews themselves and their wives are not allowed to wear costly dress with gold chains, nor cloth of gold and silver, nor silver, ornaments on belts." The traditional Jewish dress (black bekeshe and caftan) and hair styles differing from the Christians (luxuriant beard and sidelocks) appeared in Poland probably as late as the 16th century.

In Jewish quarters and towns, social and religious life focused on the prayer-houses. In the majority of communities the synagogue was not only the place where services were conducted twice a day. Its facilities were also employed for a variety of other purposes. It served as the meeting place for the male population and the leaders of the community, and the kahal court trials. In larger towns special buildings called the Jewish town halls were erected housing a prison for those who were sentenced by kahal courts, that is debtors, thieves, brawlers and those who were found to violate ritual prescriptions. Next to the prayer-house stood the yeshiva, hospital, a ritual bath (steaming room) and separately a mikveh or the baths for women.

Streets in Jewish towns were narrow, densely built up and generally lacking pavements and sewers. From time to time epidemics broke out which decimated the population and fires were a frequent occurence since they spread very quickly because of timber building. Brick structures appeared in the Jewish quarters of larger cities as late as the end of the 16th century, for example in Lvov, Cracow and Poznań. In view of the limited area of the Jewish quarters, congestion increased with the growth in number of the population. One house accommodated several, and sometimes over ten, families who nestled in its small rooms divided from one another by thin walls. Only the most wealthy had flats of several rooms while the poorest lived usually in the basements and attics.

The furnishings of the Jewish flats did not differ much from those in the Christian homes and depended above all on the wealth of the owner. The elements which made Jewish flats different were the mezuzot (a parchment scroll with quotations from the Bible and *Shaddai,* an ancient name of God, written on it), which every Jew had attached to the right-hand doorpost of his home, liturgical vessels and rabbinical books bound in leather. There were also more pots and pans since according to the Jewish ritual there had to be separate plates and pots for meat and milk dishes. The wealthier homes also had a separate set of pesah dishes, while in the poorer ones before the pesah everyday dishes were cleaned by scalding them in boiling water.

The routine of everyday life changed on Saturdays and holidays. On Saturdays the grown-ups spent the morning in the prayer-house and the following meal was more substantial than usual. In the afternoon the host set to studying the Bible or the Talmud, while the women read romances or women's Bibles which included legends and fables.

The most important holidays were Yom Kippur (the Day of Atonement), Sukkoth or Sukkot (the Feast of Booths), Pesah (the Passover), Hanukkah or Chanukah (the Feast of Dedication or the Feast of Lights), Rosh ha-Shanah (the New Year) and Purim (the Feast of Lots). In the celebrations of these festivals one can discern not only the sources of religious emotions and mystical experience but also an important element of social community. The community of common prayer was among the followers of the Mosaic religion very strong. This is what for centuries has joined together Jews all over the world. The Jewish festivals combined traditional and sacral elements with ethical and historical experience. The celebration of religious rites inspired folk artists and contributed to the development of various forms of artistic expression and aesthetic sensitivity, for such festivities called for a special artistic background, for music and singing.

The ritual of Jewish holidays has not changed much since the 16th—18th centuries, with the only difference that the Purim celebrated on the 14th and 15th day of the month of Adar (turn of February and March) and which was to commemorate the events described in the Book of Esther, was more joyous and ceremonious in olden days than in later periods. During these festivities relations and friends visited each other, sent good wishes and exchanged gifts. Special cakes in the form of triangles were baked called Haman's ears and young people held parties and masquerades. In some communities, especially in Western Poland, young people prepared theatricals about, for example, the story of Mordecai and Esther or other biblical themes.

The birth of a child and circumcision were celebrated in Jewish families in a special way. The bed of the mother was decorated and guests were served sweetmeats and wine. On the night before the ceremony of circumcision of a new born baby, women kept watch in the room of the mother. The purpose was not so much looking after her as, according to the convictions prevailing in the era of the spreading Kabbalah, the guarding of the baby against witches and evil spirits.

Until the age of three, boys were brought up exclusively by parents. From four years of age part of these duties were taken over by school. Girls, on the other hand, were brought up at home until they were married and in the meantime they were taught the duties of future house-wives. For girls aged twelve and boys aged thirteen special coming-of-age festivities were held. Particularly grand was the *bar mitzvah,* that is the day on which a thirteen year old boy began to take part in common prayer in the synagogue together with the adults.

Marriages were contracted at an early age, usually eighteen for boys and between twelve and fourteen for girls. Marriages were arranged by a match-maker (*shadkhan*) and the interested parties were not asked for agreement. The richer girls were given a dowry from their parents while the poor ones were supplied by the kahal from a special "women's fund".

Marriages and weddings usually took place in the courtyards of the synagogue in the open air. In richer families wedding ceremonies were held in private homes, with great pomp, dancing and music, while poor families held their wedding parties in the so-called *tanzhausen,* or dance houses, which were to be found in nearly every community. Dancing was to the tunes played by a Jewish band.

Christian public opinion generally maintained that Jewish marriages were very happy, though Jews themselves sometimes voiced the view that they were contracted too early in life.

ILLNESS AND FUNERALS

In case of illness assistance was given by Jewish doctors or barber-surgeons. Rarely did the Jews apply for help to a Christian doctor. The poor could count on assistance from the kahals which paid the wages of hospital personnel and hired barber-surgeons to apply leeches.

In contrast to the weddings, funerals were very modest and usually took place on the day of death or a day after. Prayers were said at the cemetery. All ministrations connected with the burying of the corpse were performed by the holy brotherhoods, the so-called *Hevra Kaddisha,* which exacted high payment for their services from the rich Jews with part of the proceeds destined for financing the funerals of the poorest folk.

POLISH JEWRY
IN THE 19TH AND 20TH CENTURIES

Polish Jews entered the 19th century as a community differing from the other citizens of the divided country in their speech, customs and religion but also with a different legal position defined in the statutes of each of the partitioning states and the short-lived Duchy of Warsaw (1807—15) created by Napoleon. The laws valid in Polish territory, derived from the period of the Commonwealth, laid down the different position of each estate: the gentry, the clergy, the burghers and the peasants. The place of Jews in society was defined in separate laws and thus they formed a closed group, another independent estate.

The foreign partitioning powers introduced many changes to these laws, for the most part to the detriment of their Jewish populations as compared with their status in independent Poland. During the 19th century, together with the decline and liquidation of feudal relations in all partition zones, gradual emancipation of Jews was taking place. This process was closely connected with the social liberation aims of the remaining groups of the population.

In the Austrian ruled part of Poland the basic legal norms concerning the Jews were introduced in the late 18th century. They restricted the number of occupations the Jews were allowed to perform (for example they were forbidden to be chemists, brewers or flour-millers), the possibilities of engaging in trade were limited and some of the Jews were forced to move from country to towns. It should be added that some towns still enjoyed the privilege of *de non tolerandis Judaeis,* for example Biała, Jasło, Wieliczka and Żywiec, while in others the occupation authorities enclosed the Jews in special quarters, for example in Lvov, Nowy Sącz and Tarnów. These new regulations, which were introduced as a "progressive reform", contributed to the worsening of the living conditions of a large part of Jewish society. According to estimates, in the 1820's in Galicia over forty per cent of all Jews had no permanent employment thus forming the proletariat who lived "from the air" (*Luftmenshen*).

These restrictions applied above all to the poor strata whom the Austrian authorities thought to be a troublesome element. On the other hand, rich entrepreneurs enjoyed a relatively wide scope of freedom of activity. Thus this policy led to the intensification of material and social differences among the Jews themselves. While individuals managed to acquire riches, the overwhelming majority lived in poverty.

Mention should be made of the important role played by Jewish merchants in Galicia. Major trade centres were Lvov and Brody. The latter became a large commercial centre in Central Europe owing to its convenient situation across communication routes and also thanks to it acquiring, in the first half of the 19th century, customs privileges which promoted trade with Russia.

Basic changes in the situation of Galician Jewry took place after 1848. Jews were active in the revolutionary movement of the period, which resulted in a Polish-Jewish reconciliation and Jewish emancipation. And although these privileges were abolished in the following years, from 1859 on the Austrian authorities began gradually to repeal legal restrictions. In 1867—68 all citizens, Jews included, were finally made equal in the eyes of the law.

As a result of the difficult economic conditions of Galicia, situated as it was at the peripheries of the Habsburg monarchy, equal right was not enough to solve many everyday problems. Economic conditions forced many more enterprising people to emigrate. Generally Jews from Galicia sought work in other countries of the Austro-Hungarian Empire, sometimes in Vienna, and also in Hungary and the Balkan countries. Towards the end of the 19th century the swelling wave of peasant emigration overseas drew in many Jews as well. Between 1881 and 1900 some 150,000 Jews emigrated, while between 1900 and 1914 about 175,000 Jews from Galicia left for the United States alone.

The Prussian laws introduced in former Polish territories were also directed against the Jewish proletariat. There were a number of restrictions which, among other things, aimed at forcing the Jews out of the country as long as they could not produce evidence of possessing appropriate wealth. The General Ordinance on the Jews (*General-Judenreglement*) of 17 April 1797 divided all Jews into those "protected"(*Schutzjuden)*, who were obliged to know the German language and possess a definite wealth, and those merely "tolerated". This ordinance limited the Jews' right to settle in the countryside and also ordered the removal from the state of those Jews who could not prove their right to living in a given town on the territory of the partition zone at the time when this territory had been annexed to Prussia. The same regulations were introduced in the Grand Duchy of Poznań which had been part of the Duchy of Warsaw before the former was joined to Prussia.

Equal rights for all Jews came only with the year of revolutions, 1848, when the differences between the two categories of Jews were abolished. Later, in 1850, Jews were given the same rights as the remaining subjects of the king of Prussia. It should be added incidentally that the legislation which accorded certain privileges to those Jews who spoke German was conducive to their language and national assimilation. On the other hand, a large number of those who could not speak German, had to leave the country.

The constitution of the Duchy of Warsaw, by abolishing differences between the estates, introduced formal equality of all citizens. In spite of this, it provided for a number of restrictions in relation to Jews. For example they were forbidden to work in certain occupations and the granting of full rights to them was made dependent on their cultural and traditional assimilation. Around the Jewish question discussion broke out. Some authors accused them of selling cheap, poor quality products. To this the outstanding economist, Wawrzyniec Surowiecki (1769—1827) replied: "It is not the fault of the merchant or the craftsman that he supplies the country with this sort [of goods], but it is the result of the poverty and misery of the inhabitants who can afford nothing better. Were this sentence not true in relation to Poland, the Jews, together with their humble goods, would have soon gone bankrupt." In such discussions one could easily discern interests of the burghers who were afraid of competition from Jewish merchants and craftsmen and therefore were in favour of certain restrictive measures against the Jews.

The overwhelming majority of Jews in the Duchy of Warsaw were poor and made their living from petty trade and crafts. Only some succeeded in accumulating fortunes. Of the latter, the leading place undoubtedly goes to the family of Samuel Zbitkover (1756—1801) who laid the foundations of his fortune in the final years of the Commonwealth when he was engaged in provisioning the army. Then there was also the banker Samuel Kronenberg whose son would play an important role in the country's economic and political life.

The Congress of Vienna of 1815 resolved to create from the larger part of the Duchy of Warsaw a new political entity — the constitutional Kingdom of Poland (also known as Congress Poland), with the Russian tsar as its king. Although the constitution provided for equality of all citizens, this referred only to the Christians while Jews were deprived of both citizens' and civil rights. The legal norms from the period of the Duchy of Warsaw were kept in force. Jews were not encompassed by the general duty of army services instead of which they were burdened with heavy taxes. In cities the Jewish population had no municipal rights. Only certain forms of Jewish self-government were preserved. From the highly complex system of autonomous self-governing organizations of Jewish society in old Poland, only the lowest rung, the community, was left. In 1821 new regulations replaced the former kahal boards with new prayer-house supervisory bodies. The latter's terms of reference were limited only to religious matters and charity campaigns. They were also entrusted with certain administrative functions, for example the collecting of recruitment taxes.

Important changes, connected with the process of social differentiation, took place within Jewish society. This process took on a particularly clear-cut form in the country's capital, Warsaw, where there arose a group of rich business owners and numerous intelligentsia, the latter composed for the most part of representatives of the professions (doctors, lawyers) as well as artists and booksellers, since Jews were not employed in public offices and institutions. These groups kept in touch with the corresponding Polish groups and took an active part in the country's intellectual life and political movements. Gradually they also came closer to the Polish groups as regards dress, customs and language. They began to aspire to full citizens' rights and emancipation and the transformation of the Jewish community as a whole. They sought ways of reforming the traditional customs, adapting the various religious requirements and prescriptions to the conditions of contemporary life and freeing themselves from the domination of the intolerant, and sometimes downright primitive, orthodox circles. Jewish youth formed secret societies collaborating with their Polish counterparts in clandestine educational and political work.

The November Insurrection of 1830—31 did not change the legal status of the Jews. The conservative leaders of the insurrection did not plan very progressive reforms in any field of social life. Nevertheless since Jews in Warsaw shared the national liberation aims of the insurrection, in early 1831 small groups of the richest Jewish sections were allowed to join the National Guards. Representatives of the petite bourgeoisie could enlist in the Municipal Guards while the proletariat joined the Security Guards.

After the collapse of the November Insurrection the first steps were made to introduce in the Kingdom of Poland the same rights as those binding in the rest of the Russian Empire in relation to Jews. Also in this field the Russian authorities attempted to blur out the differences between the Polish partition zone and the rest of Russia, although the administrative separateness of the Kingdom of Poland and its self-governing bodies were preserved for the time being. Various tendencies clashed. Only a few people managed to win for themselves personal privileges which freed them from certain obligations.

The national authorities opposed unification attempts and tried to keep in force separate laws for the Jews. On the other hand progressive circles were preparing projects for granting Jews equal rights. The latter attempts corresponded to those represented by the progressive enlightened Jewish circles. It is true that arguments and discussions did not produce any direct effect in the form of definite laws, but they promoted cooperation between those Jewish and Polish circles who wanted the abolition of legal and economic elements of the feudal system which still prevailed in the Kingdom of Poland. Next to the enfranchisement of the peasants, the most important question was the granting of equal rights to the Jews.

Political movements became particularly active in 1861. Young Jews joined the various underground circles which arose in many towns. In summer news reached Poland about the death of two outstanding and much esteemed Polish emigration leaders, Joachim Lelewel (1786—1861) and Prince Adam Czartoryski (1770—1861). Prayers in commemoration of these two famous Poles were held in churches with the participation of Jews and in synagogues with the participation of Poles. Joint manifestations were organized on anniversaries of important historic events. The famous rabbi Dov Berush Meisels (1798—1870), who had moved from Cracow to Warsaw, proclaimed the brotherhood of Poles and Jews.

During these lively events, the decree, which had been long discussed, on elections to county and municipal self-governing bodies was announced. The right to vote was granted to all male citizens over 25 years of age who could speak and write Polish, irrespective of religion, but with the introduction of a high property qualification. By this decree for the first time Jews were allowed to take part in elections on an equal footing with the rest of society. Jewish representatives were elected to local self-governing bodies.

In the autumn of 1861 further demonstrations took place. For example on 10 October, during the funeral of Archbishop Antoni Fijałkowski (1778—1861), three graduates of the Warsaw rabbinical school unfurled the Polish banner. Patriotic manifestations with the participation of Jews were held also in other towns. Soon reprisals followed.

In these circumstances the Russian authorities decided to approve the principles of reform of the legal status of Jews, which had been prepared by the autonomous organs of the Kingdom of Poland. On 5 June 1862 the decree introducing equal rights in many important fields was announced. Thus the road to gradual emancipation was opened.

Since the most politically-minded Jewish circles considered the decree as their victory, they supported the January Insurrection of 1863. Several months after the outbreak of the insurrection, the insurrectionary National Government proclaimed full equality of rights for Jews in Poland. Jews found themselves in the ranks of insurrectionary armies and also among the leaders of the insurrection. The well-known banker and industrialist, Leopold Kronenberg (1812—78), who had wide-ranging contacts in European banking circles, organized the insurrection's finances and won credits. The fall of the insurrection, however, crushed hopes and ruined the reforms of the National Government.

The progress which took place in introducing equal rights for Jews in the 1860's favoured the development of cultural and political life and transformations in consciousness. In the second half of the 19th century, main political currents took shape. They had their supporters not only among the relatively limited wealthy social strata and intelligentsia, but also among the masses of the population.

Already in the previous decades a movement aimed at the emancipation of Jews developed. One important component was aiming at their "reform", which meant making them similar in dress and customs to their Polish surroundings and animating their intellectual life. Some of the leading representatives of this movement gradually became assimilated into Polish society. For them assimilation was the aim to which Jewish society as a whole should aspire. Though they preserved their links with their old circles, their children considered themselves, and were considered by others, to be Poles. These sections of Jewish society produced many families which played an important role in Polish culture, for example the Słonimskis, Natansons and Toeplitzs.

The programme of assimilation found it hard to reach to the masses of the population, one of the reasons being that the latter had no access to schools other than religious ones and had no conditions for mastering the Polish language and adopting different customs. What is more, after the basic premises of emancipation were won, the programme of assimilation ceased to be considered as the only way to social emancipation. Other political concepts appealed to the masses much more.

Towards the end of the 19th century another factor also emerged. Throughout Europe a wave of nationalism, directed above all against the Jews, swelled. France saw the Dreyfus case in 1894, in Czechoslovakia there was the Hilsner case in 1899 and in Russia the Beylis case in 1913. In Germany Richard Wagner wrote: "The liberation from the yoke of Judaism is for us the supreme necessity." In the Kingdom of Poland this current was represented by Roman Dmowski (1864—1939) and the National Democratic Party created by him.

The medium for anti-semitic sentiments was the growing rivalry among the petite bourgeoisie. In Warsaw and other towns appeals to boycott Jewish shops appeared and instances of raids on Jewish shops were noted. The writer and journalist Leo Belmont (1865—1941) wrote: "In some shops the eloquent notice 'Christian shop' appeared in accordance with the recommendation of Mr. Roman Dmowski who is the author of a new commentary to the Gospels, namely that Christ cleansed the Temple of the Jewish money-lenders only in order to bring the Polish tradesmen in there." And although the progressive Polish circles opposed such tendencies, they could do nothing to prevent them. This situation contributed to the defeat of the assimilation movement as the political concept which would help Jews win for themselves mass influence in society.

The difficult economic situation, discrimination practised by the Russian authorities and finally the emergence of anti-semitism gave rise to Jewish emigration. They departed for some West European countries but above all for the United States. In most cases, however, they preserved strong sentimental links with their home country.

Towards the end of the 19th century, among the Jewish proletariat, some groups of the impovershed petite bourgeoisie and part of the intelligentsia, great influence was exerted by the ideologies of the workers' parties. Later a Zionist movement emerged and finally the conservative movement took on organized forms. Other groups and movements had much lesser influence.

The above mentioned political and ideological movements were not fully uniform. The workers' parties were divided as far as their strategies and tactics were concerned. Also as well as the organizations which accepted members irrespective of nationality, there were some which had a strictly national character. Among the Jewish proletariat strong influence was exerted by the Jewish socialist Bund party formed at a secret meeting in Vilna in 1897. The Bund members proclaimed that it was possible to solve the social and nationality problems of the Jews in their countries of residence, that is also in Polish territories. Considerable influence was also won by the party called Po'alei Zion (Workers of Zion) divided into a left and right wing. Many Jews were members of the Social Democratic Party of the Kingdom of Poland and Lithuania. Within the Polish Socialist Party a Jewish Organization existed which produced many outstanding leaders.

The workers' movement aimed at the solution of nationality problems through the transformation of the existing social system and the liquidation of exploitation of man by man which was inherent in the capitalist system. A different stand was taken by the Zionist movement which put to the fore the nationality question. It maintained that this question could not be solved by way of cooperation of working people irrespective of their nationality. It treated the nationality conflicts as an unavoidable phenomenon and saw the only hope in the foundation of a Jewish state in Palestine. The realization of this goal was to be the main task of each Jew, although it was also necessary to defend one's interests within the country of residence. The Zionist movement, too, was divided as regards concepts concerning its strategy and tactics.

For the conservatives, the most important problem was the preservation of tradition identified with religion and the scrupulous observance of customs. This was accompanied by considerable indifference towards other matters. In relation to authorities their programme principle was the attitude of loyalty, and thus they proclaimed full obedience to state laws. Thus far they had not formed their own political organization and their influence was based on the authority of the zaddikim and the faithful hasidim who formed their courts.

In 1918 some groups of the Jewish population, especially the conservative circles which maintained a detached attitude in relation to problems which did not concern the Jews directly, took a position of neutrality and expectation on the question of the rebirth of the Polish state. Some were afraid of any change since — as the experience of many generations had taught them — changes usually brought disaster in their wake. This opinion seemed to be justified in view of the anti-Jewish riots and raids which took place in some parts of the country, although the real significance of these events must not be overestimated. They were caused by conflicts of a social and economic nature between the merchant stratum and its customers from small towns and the countryside. In other instances these were simply criminal offences, for example in Lvov where the pogroms in the Jewish streets were the work of criminals released from prisons.

The conservatives, represented by the orthodox party Agudat Israel, which was founded in Poland in 1916, declared their loyalty to the Polish state shortly after its government was constituted. On the other hand representatives of other directions, especially the socialist organizations and their like, very often demonstrated their positive attitude to the independence of Poland and also took an active part in the struggle for liberation. Jews found themselves in the ranks of the Legions organized by Józef Piłsudski (1867—1935) and also in other volunteer formations which proclaimed the programme of independent Poland.

Such attitude to the approaching transformations was connected with the conviction — maintained by both the Polish and Jewish masses — that the re-emergent Polish state would have a truly democratic character and thus would bring a solution of the urgent social and political problems and become a state of social justice for the working people.

Poland emerged as a bourgeois republic under the influence of the great revolutionary movement which swept the whole of Eastern and Central Europe in the years 1917—19. Although the reborn state did not solve the basic economic and social questions, its legislation granted equal rights to all citizens irrespective of nationality and religious convictions. This was guaranteed by its constitution adopted by the Seym in March 1921. Thus were abolished the legal norms inherited from the partitioning powers, which gave different legal status to various groups of society. However some questions as laid down in the constitution lent themselves to various interpretations. In 1931 the Seym passed a law which abrogated expressis verbis all regulations which were discriminatory on grounds of religion, nationality and race. In this respect independent Poland fulfilled the people's hopes.

The matter was different in the field of economic relations. In the inter-war period Poland found herself in an extremely difficult situation. Leaving aside the fluctuations of economic development experienced by all capitalist countries (a particularly deep drop in production, employment and incomes was noted in the first half of the 1930's), the average increase in the number of places of work was far behind the population growth. Overpopulation of the countryside became more acute, which in turn brought about the shrinking of the internal market and the resultant impoverishment of petty tradesmen and craftsmen. Unemployment in towns took on catastrophic dimensions. In these circumstances, especially in the 1930's, the pauperization of those strata which earned their living from small shops increased. Economists spoke of the overcrowding of trade and crafts.

According to the 1931 census of the nearly 32 million Polish citizens, 10 per cent (or some three million) were Jews. Of this figure 42 per cent worked in industry, mining and crafts and 36 per cent in trade and kindred branches. Other occupations played a lesser role in the Jews' occupational structure. In some branches of the economy Jews constituted a majority. This concerned above all the retail trade where 71 per cent of all tradesmen were Jewish. In the clothing and leather industry this percentage was almost 50. Typical Jewish occupations were tailoring and shoe-making. However in the conditions of massive unemployment, in spite of the over-abundance of certain specialities in crafts, they had no chance of finding employment. At the same time there was a growth in the number of merchants and craftsmen of other nationalities. In the countryside, the expanding cooperative movement became a serious rival to the private merchants.

It would be wrong to assume that the concentration of Jews in certain branches of the economy and their pauperization were the result of a deliberate policy on the part of the state. It is true that the administration was unfavourably disposed towards employing other than Polish nationals in state enterprises, especially those of military importance (for example railways and armaments factories) and therefore removed Jews from these establishments. However, the direct reason for anti-Jewish discrimination has to be sought in the past, in the relations which had been formed in the period of the partitions. The overcoming of the traditional occupational and social structure of the Jewish community could be accomplished only by the acceleration of the economic development of the country as a whole and also by the creation of conditions favouring the acquiring of new trades which had not been popular among the Jewish community. This problem was also perceived by some Jewish organizations which undertook actions aimed at training young people in various specialities. This was done most often by the Zionist organizations which in connection with their Palestinian plans attempted to prepare groups of settlers having definite trades. However the scope of this action was very modest indeed since it depended on winning financial means as well as those willing to go to Palestine. Similar undertakings could not be carried out on a mass scale without appropriate assistance from the state in a situation where the government found it difficult to acquire sufficient financial resources for the most urgent needs. What is more, even if money had been available, the specialists trained in this way would not have been able to find employment anyway.

The same objective reasons made it impossible to overcome the concentration of Jewish labourers in small enterprises and workshops, while it should be borne in mind that over 70 per cent of the Jewish urban proletariat were employed in such small establishments.

This adverse situation was also affected by some traditional customs and religion. Since Jews observed Sabbath, it was difficult to employ in one enterprise both Jewish and Christian workers without disorganizing the rhythm of production. Even Jewish entrepreneurs unwillingly employed a Jewish labour force. Of course not all of them were Orthodox Jews and not all of them refused to work on Saturdays. However those who wanted to work on Saturdays were treated with suspicion by their employers who feared lest they belonged to a socialist or communist organization and one day might organize the factory work force in struggle for their interests. In smaller establishments, in which the owner himself took part in both the production process and management, work on Saturdays was suspended.

The Jewish question in inter-war Poland was above all a social problem. Without solving the problems which were common to all working people, there was no chance of changing the lot of the Polish Jews. And the capitalist system provided no prospect of a radical overcoming of backwardness and increasing the number of jobs, despite efforts on the part of the state undertaken in particular in the second half of the 1930's.

Thus emigration continued. There are no exhaustive data on this subject. However, it is known that between 1927 and 1938 nearly 200,000 Polish Jews left Poland, of which number 74,000 went to Palestine, 34,000 to Argentina and 28,000 to the United States. The largest waves of emigration were recorded in the 1920's. Following the great slump, after 1929, those countries which up till then accepted immigrants, introduced new, ever more severe restrictions on immigration. This concerned, among other countries, the United States. For this reason in the 1930's overseas emigration became limited in scope while the number of those going to Palestine increased. According to the most reliable calculations, between 1919 and 1942 almost 140,000 Polish Jews went to Palestine, that is, some 42 per cent of the total number of immigrants accepted by that country; the largest intensification of Palestine-bound emigration took place in the years 1933—36 when the number of emigrants amounted to 75,000.

In the difficult economic situation and the changes in legal and political status of Jews after Poland had regained her independence, various programmes of activity were formed. The traditional programme of the Agudat Israel, which boiled down to the observance of religious prescriptions, loyalty towards the state and the expectation of the Kingdom of God, could not suffice. Although the position of this party among the petite bourgeoisie was maintained by the authority of the zaddikim (a particularly important role in the leadership of the Agudat Israel was played by the famous zaddik of Góra Kalwaria who was however criticized by many), its attempts at consolidating a specific kind of ideological ghetto (the isolation of the Jews from the goim) resulted in a gradual decrease of its influence. Step by step the party moved towards the acceptance of the prospect of building a Jewish state in Palestine.

On the other hand, the influence of the workers' parties continued to be strong. The most important role was still played by the Bund, some concepts of which were close to those of the radical left wing, though its members represented a whole variety of views. The Bund differed from the programme put forwad by the communists in that it demanded cultural and national autonomy for national minorities, especially for the Jews, and perceived the necessity of organizing the whole of the Jewish proletariat in one, separate national party. Many Bund leaders saw the need for dictatorship by the proletariat (the Bund programme adopted in 1930 mentioned the possibility of such dictatorship). The party was decidedly opposed to the conservatives and discarded religion. It accused the Agudat Israel of defending the interests of the propertied classes to the detriment of the needs of the masses. The most outstanding leaders of the Bund were Victor Alter (1890—1941), Henryk Erlich (1882—1941) and Samuel Zygelbojm (1895—1943).

The Bund, like the illegal Communist Party of Poland to which many Jews also belonged and the Polish Socialist Party, saw the only chance of solving the Jewish question in Poland in building a socialist society without man's exploitation by man. It sought its allies among workers of all nationalities living in Poland. It opposed all concepts of emigration since it perceived the impracticability of the idea of organizing emigration of a several million strong nation. The socialist leaders considered the Palestinian campaign to be an element weakening the forces of the proletariat fighting for a change in social relations and as a solution which at best could constitute a chance for only few.

A radical social programme was also voiced by the left wing of the Po'alei Zion which saw prospects for the Jews in a socialist revolution and in introducing cultural and national autonomy. For the future, it accepted the idea of building a socialist Jewish state in Palestine and therefore it supported the Palestinian campaigns. Its leading members were Antoni Buchsbaum, Szachna Sagan and Józef Witkin-Zerubavel (1876—1912). A much smaller following was enjoyed by the right wing of the Po'alei Zion which concentrated above all on Palestinian works, that is all activity aimed at forming a future Jewish state, including education of qualified farmers, workers and soldiers.

All the workers' organizations, irrespective of the differences that separated them, cooperated in many important issues. They undertook a common struggle against campaigns organized by the right wing of the National Democratic Party. In Warsaw they even formed an underground organization the task of which was to put up armed resistance to the nationalist militants. Both Jews and Poles connected with the workers' movement took part in its work.

Different views were voiced by Zionist organizations which saw the Jews' future exclusively in emigration and in building their own state. The Palestinian works became the most important aim while current issues of political life were relegated to the background, though they were not totally neglected.

After Poland regained her independence, the most important organization was the Zionist Organization in Poland composed of three regional branches (for the former Austrian partition zone, eastern Galicia and western Galicia). Its members represented various views which in later years resulted in its break-up and the formation of a splinter group known as Zionist Revisionists who set up the New Zionist Organization. Among the leading activists of the Zionist movement mention is due above all to Rabbi Osias (Jehoshua) Thon (1870—1936), Emil Sommerstein (1883—1957), Henryk Rosmaryn (1882—1955), all representing the Et Livnot wing, and Yizhak Gruenbaum (1879—1970), the magnificent orator, for many years Seym deputy from the Al ha-Mishmar wing.

Zionism was strongly opposed to both the workers' and conservative movements. The latter accused them of profaning religious tradition because in the future Jewish state the language of everyday use was to be Hebrew, the language of the holy books. The other political groups generally considered Yiddish to be the language of everyday use.

It is only an apparent paradox that the Zionist movement found support in Poland's nationalist circles. In the 1930's government circles granted it some assistance, especially to the radical group of the Zionist Revisionists who were ready to win an independent Jewish state in armed struggle. The plane on which agreement was reached was the question of emigration. For the Polish government saw no chances of solving the country's social problems with the use of its own resources and wanted to stimulate the emigration of the most impoverished sections which were the heaviest burden on the labour market. In the second half of the 1930's another factor was added to this. From the National Democratic Party, the Sanacja government — the political camp which wielded dictatorial power in Poland at the time — adopted some of its ideas an tried to induce emigration first of all of national minorities.

An important arena of struggle among various political groups active among the Jews were the religious communities. The community was in principle a religious institution derived from the synagogue supervisors established in the former Russian partition zone. The principles of activity of the communities were laid down in a decree of 1927 which was binding in all of Poland with the exception of Silesia. By law, each community encompassed all followers of Judaism who lived in its area of operation. Obviously unbelievers were allowed to leave this organization and thus relinquish both the duties and the rights which were binding on its members. However, in fact only a few did that.

According to the above mentioned decree, the terms of reference of the community included the maintenance of the rabbinate, the buildings and facilities which served religious needs and cemeteries, the supervision of religious instruction of their youth, the provision of kosher meat to the faithful, the administration of the community's property and funds and dispensing of charities. The sphere of activity thus defined went beyond the limits of purely religious ministrations. The management of funds and assistance to the poor were after all of basic importance, especially in the years of economic crisis. The authorities of the community were thus responsible not only for satisfying religious needs but also for social policy. For these reasons the Jewish communities aroused interest in some political parties.

Traditionally the community boards were dominated by the Agudat Israel. However as early as the 1920's, especially in large industrial centres, the Bund and the Zionists were also represented on these bodies. During the elections held in the spring of 1931, those groups challenged the orthodox factions since they saw the possibility of transforming the denominational institutions into a kind of cultural and national self-government. In this conflict, representatives of the Agudat Israel resorted to various abuses of electoral regulations, such as depriving their opponents of the right to vote on the accusation that they were acting against the religion. They also used the assistance of administrative bodies which were afraid lest the denominational self-government might become in time a political institution. The opponents of the conservatives quite rightly maintained that in many communities the latter neglected the needs of the working masses and even accused them of corrupt practices.

The second half of the 1930's brought many phenomena which intensified emigration sentiments among the Polish Jews. The country's economic situation did not promise any improvement, while emigration could facilitate the gaining of means of subsistence. Some young Zionists grew impatient since the longed-for proclamation of a Jewish state did not materialize. Violent acts committed by the National Democrats became more frequent, despite opposition on the part of progressive organizations and many outstanding scholars. However in practice in many universities the nationalists succeeded in introducing various regulations which were aimed against students of Jewish origin (not only those who considered themselves to be Jewish). Some municipal authorities passed regulations discriminating against the Jews though formally in accord with the existing legislation. There were cases of groups of militants beating up professors (for example Professors Edward Lipiński and Tadeusz Kotarbiński) who were opposed to anti-semitism. There were also instances of pogroms in small towns where the mob, incited by the nationalists and composed mainly of criminal elements, robbed and demolished Jewish booths and shops and maltreated their owners. Assistance from the workers could not always stop the attackers. The government took an equivocal stand in this matter. Though it condemned pogroms, yet at the same time Prime Minister Felicjan Sławoj Składkowski (1885—1962) declared in the Seym: "Economic boycott? That's right!" The Church condemned such excesses, but simultaneously well-known journalists writing for Catholic journals advised Christians to stay apart from the Jews.

Of great importance were the events in Germany. After Hitler took power, mass persecutions of Jews started, among whom there were also some 50,000 Polish subjects living in Germany. This resulted in official protests from the Polish consulates and embassy which took various steps to help the persecuted. However, the Polish authorities were afraid that this persecution would reduce the Polish Jews living in Germany to such poverty that they would be forced to return to Poland where they would not find any means of subsistence. Many employees of the Polish consulates — as reports sent to Warsaw indicate — intervened on behalf of Jews for purely humanitarian reasons, since they wanted, at least to some degree, to alleviate the difficult situation of the persecuted Jews.

These interventions stopped the Third Reich from applying against the Polish Jews all repressive measures which were used against the German citizens of Jewish origin. However nothing could change radically the situation of Polish Jews in Germany. In the years 1938—39 more and more often Polish Jews, leaving behind all their property, were hurried across the border to Poland under threat of death. Particularly harsh measures were applied in the last days of October 1938 when some 13,000 were forced in this way out of Germany (according to data of the Polish consulates). For several days the victims stayed in the open air, between the two border points, before they were allowed back to Poland. Here, having no means of subsistence, they waited for many weeks in transit camps near the border.

All these events made the picture of the future really gloomy. Poland faced a direct danger. Those who were preparing for departure from Poland had one more reason for doing so. The others, the overwhelming majority, who had no such possibility nor wished to leave Poland which they considered their motherland, awaited anxiously what the future had in store for them.

In the face of threat from the Third Reich the Jewish community in Poland demonstrated great self-sacrifice in the cause of defending the Republic. They contributed to the state loan for defensive purposes and collected funds for the army. This sacrifice manifested itself also during September 1939. The outstanding scholar Emanuel Ringelblum wrote the following about the sentiments prevailing then in Warsaw: "The Warsaw Jews were overcome with enthusiasm which recalled the year 1861, the era of fraternity." During the siege of Warsaw, Jewish organizations took an active part in civil defence and assistance to victims. The historian Bernard Mark recalls an unusual demonstration of Jews through the streets of Warsaw: "In the first line there marched five well-known rabbis in long, silk black coats and sable hats... They were followed by students of the rabbinical college, each carrying a spade on his shoulders." Many Jews helped to dig earthworks even on holiday, Saturday. Others took up arms and fought the common enemy. The defeat of the Polish army in the September campaign opened a new, tragic period in the common history of Jews and Poles.

Translated by Bogna Piotrowska

PRINTERS, PUBLISHERS AND BOOKSELLERS

In writing on Jewish commerce in the old Polish territories, historians most frequently fail to perceive that the Jewish merchants and even stall-keepers were among the first to have introduced trade in books, which gave rise to the development of book printing, publishing, and editing in Poland. A Jewish salesman, travelling through towns and villages, would offer, among other goods, also books. These were mostly calendars, dream-books, guide-books, and prayerbooks for his co-religionists, but not infrequently also masterpieces of world literature, at times smuggled across several frontiers at the risk of one's life. Let us recall here Adam Mickiewicz's words:

Hence, despite tsarist threats, in the teeth of the customs officers,
The Jews smuggle volumes of my works into Lithuania.

A Jewish bookseller is also the theme of Władysław Syrokomla's poem:
...With his back to the wall
Stands a grey-bearded Jew, dressed in rags,
Blood-shot, filmy eyes, senility written on his face,
An old book under his arm. This is the doyen of the booksellers!
Don't laugh at him! It is almost fifty years
Since he took up his place by this wall
And offered pamphlets and trash to the passers-by.
In exchange for a copper coin, he gave golden learning.

The Jews were a book-loving people. The renowned centres of production and sale of Hebrew books, and from the 19th century also books in Yiddish, included not only Amsterdam, Venice, Vienna, or Prague, but also Lublin, Cracow, Vilna, and Warsaw. In many countries, Jews came to be publishers and distributors not only of Jewish literature, but also the literature of the country of their residence. In this respect, Jews had played a particular role in the Polish territories.

From the earliest times, there had been a considerable demand for Hebrew books, above all for prayer-books of various kinds, the Bible, the books of the Talmud, etc., resulting from the fact that they were indispensable for the religious life and synagogue ritual and that among the Jews, or at least among men, there were no illiterates — everybody could read prayers. The demand for these books in the Polish lands was satisfied primarily by imports, but also by local printing offices functioning from the 16th century. In Cracow, for example, an unknown printer published, in 1530—31, the Pentateuch and Haggadah, while the Halicz brothers brought out several prayer-books for holy days, so called *Mahzorim*. Elyakum Halicz, even after he had been christened and had taken the name of Johannes, continued bringing out Hebrew books.

Lublin was also one of the oldest centres of Hebrew printing. In 1536, the printer Hayyim Schwartz published *Mahzor* with a Polish text next to the Hebrew. The second half of the 16th century witnessed the publication of a considerable number of prayer-books for weekdays (*Siddurim*) and for holy days (*Mahzorim*). The 17th and 18th centuries saw the development of Hebrew printing also in other towns, including Vilna, Grodno, and Lvov, as well as in many smaller places. The publications comprised, next to the indispensable prayer-books, volumes of the Talmud with commentaries, kabbalistic works, ethical books, etc.

As compared with other towns, in Warsaw Hebrew printing did not develop until much later. The reason for this was that Jews were not allowed to settle there. Consequently, Jewish printing offices first used to be set up in the vicinity of Warsaw. In 1775, Lazar Icchak, called Izakowicz of Krotoszyn, was the first to seek permission to open a printing office in Warsaw. A year later, King Stanislaus Augustus granted him the privilege of establishing a printing firm in Golędzinów and publishing Hebrew books and later calendars. It is worth mentioning that Hebrew books were brought out by non-Jewish printers as well, among them such renowned 18th-century publishers as Piotr Dufour and Johann Anton Krieger. The latter, having purchased the Hebrew printing offices of Hershel Leibowitz and Szmul Segal in Korzec, moved them to Nowy Dwór, where he set up a large and important centre of Hebrew book production. The Krieger firm prospered until 1818. Its efficiency is testified to by the fact that at a fair in Łęczno in 1789, it offered for sale 2,641 Hebrew books and 2,000 Jewish calendars.

In 1814, Hirsch Nossonowitz and Avigdor Lebensohn founded, in Żabia Street, Warsaw's first Jewish printing office. Soon afterwards, a Hebrew type foundry came into being. In the mid-19th century, 33 printing offices were functioning in Warsaw, including 13 Hebrew, among them the firms of Herz Schriftgiesser, Hersz Bomberg (both from 1834), Aron Kleif, Samuel Zysberg, and Abraham Baumberg.

Aside from Hebrew printers and publishers, Warsaw also had Jewish firms which were active on the Polish-language publishing market. It is worth mentioning that Jews owned about 40 per cent of all printing houses in the Kingdom of Poland, and in some towns, e. g. in Łódź and Vilna, as many as 60 per cent.

There were even whole families engaged in the printing trade. The most prominent included pioneers of Polish book publishing: the Glücksbergs and the Orgelbrands.

The first reports of the Glücksberg family, which probably had settled in the Polish territories much earlier, date from the mid-17th century and concern Emmanuel Mayer Glücksberg. Three of his sons engaged in the book trade, the best-known of them having been Mayer Nathan, also called Michał or Mikołaj (1770—1831).

In an article published in the journal *Kłosy* in 1868 and presenting the difficulties facing writers until not long ago, we read: "Such a state of the book movement in Poland had continued until almost 1820, when the bookseller and publisher, Nathan Glücksberg, appeared." Nathan and his brother

Jan were the first publishers and booksellers in the Polish territories to finance works by Polish authors and the first to introduce honoraria. By 1831, the Nathan Glücksberg firm had brought out over 220 titles. It also published magazines, among them *Gazeta Literacka*, edited by Adam Tomasz Chłędowski, director of the National Library; *Magazyn Powszechny — Dziennik Użytecznych Wiadomości* (from 1834), illustrated with woodcuts imported from abroad; and *Bronisława czyli Pamiętnik Polek* (from 1822), a women's magazine. Nathan Glücksberg was a member of a Masonic Lodge. He belonged to the leadership of the progressive Polish Jews, the so-called 26 fathers of enlightened families, advocates of assimilation with "the nation among which they are living". Of his eight children, four sons chose their father's occupation. August Emanuel Glücksberg (1804—94) published, inter alia, a four-volume *Universal Encyclopaedia* and Michał Baliński's *History of Poland,* and Nathan's brother, Jan (1784—1859) brought out *A Guide to Warsaw* (1827). Jan Glücksberg was also the publisher of many Polish journals. He took part in the November Insurrection. He was a member of the Tutelar Council of the Jewish Hospital and secretary of the Advisory Chamber for Jews in Poland.

The first reference to another prominent family of Jewish publishers, the Orgelbrands, dates from the 18th century and says that Chaim Juda Orgelbrand, married to Anna Jud, engaged in bookselling. Their son Samuel, born in 1810, founded, in Nowiniarska Street in Warsaw in 1837, a bookshop and shortly thereafter a printing house. He initially published books of adventure and romances, which activity brought him a fortune. In the middle of the 19th century, his firm employed 160 persons, and the printing works was equipped with most modern installations, including its own type foundry, stereotype room, etc. In 1858, Samuel Orgelbrand commenced a giant, pioneering work on the publication of the *Universal Encyclopaedia*. To this end, he employed some of the most outstanding Polish scholars and writers of the time. After 10 years, in spite of tremendous, chiefly financial, difficulties (the initial number of 3,000 subscribers dropped to 500), he brought the work to an end with the 28th and last volume. The encyclopaedia — the only one to have been completed in Poland in the 19th century — cost the publisher about 120,000 roubles, including 42,000 roubles in honoraria which provided many Polish scholars and writers with means of subsistence. By 1912, three abridged and corrected versions of the work, commonly called the *Orgelbrand Encyclopaedia*, had appeared. Samuel Orgelbrand published a total of about 600 titles, including 100 in Hebrew, among them the books of the Mishnah and the Gemara and the monumental 20-volume work the *Babylonian Talmud.* After his death, the firm was taken over by his sons, Hipolit and Mieczysław, and further prospered, employing already about 600 persons.

At the same time, Samuel's brother, Maurycy, a graduate — like Samuel — of the Warsaw rabbinical school, was running a printing firm in Vilna. Among his accomplishments was the publication of a great *Polish Dictionary* with 108,000 entries. During the January Insurrection, Maurycy's wife, Eleonora née Starkman, was arrested and sent into exile, where Maurycy voluntarily accompanied her. Having returned in 1873, he founded in Warsaw a large publishing company which comprised such well-known firms as Gebethner and Wolff and Michał Glücksberg.

Aside from these two, doubtless most outstanding families in the history of Polish book printing and editing, many other families won renown, among them the Merzbachs, the Natansons, Salomon Lewenthal, Gabriel Centnerszwer, and Józef Unger.

As regards the Merzbachs, we know that there was a Henryk Merzbach living with his family in Poznań in the 18th century. His sons were well-known booksellers: Ludwik (1820—90) stayed in Poznań, while Samuel Henryk (d. 1874) and Zygmunt (1801—52) moved to Warsaw, where they opened, in Miodowa Street, a bookshop along with a reading-room and a lending library. His bookshop was a meeting place for writers, poets, and bibliophiles. Samuel took part in the Polish patriotic movements. In his bookshop, prohibited publications were available. He brought out Polish and foreign books, including novels by Walter Scott. In 1833, he published three illustrated volumes of Adam Mickiewicz's poetry, and in 1857—58 an eight-volume *Selected Writings*, so far the only illustrated edition of the writings of the great poet. Merzbach's catalogues, appearing regularly from 1831 until 1874, are proof of his immensely important and versatile editing and publishing activity. Samuel's nephew and the son of Zygmunt Merzbach, Henryk, a poet, writer, and publicist, had for some time run his uncle's firm, until in 1862 he and Ludwik Polak founded, in Krakowskie Przedmieście Street, a bookshop which also sold music scores. The bookshop was frequented by writers, musicians, and political activists. In 1863, following the publication of an anti-tsarist pamphlet, the bookshop was closed down. Henryk Merzbach, in order to avoid arrest, left for Dresden and later for Brussels, where he carried on his patriotic and publishing activity. He was regarded to be one of the leaders of the Polish exiles. He was also book purveyor to King Leopold II. While in Belgium, he published, inter alia, *The Last Years of the Life of J. Lelewel* (1889).

Henryk Natanson (1820—95), a Warsaw banker and, at the same time, bookseller and publisher, was descended from an old plutocratic Jewish family. One of the seven sons of Wolf Zelig Natanson, Henryk, having graduated from the Warsaw rabbinical school and undergone training in the F. A. Brockhaus bookshop in Leipzig and the J. Zawadzki bookshop in Vilna, founded, in 1846, his own bookshop in Krakowskie Przedmieście Street. Next to trading in books imported from abroad, Natanson also conducted publishing activity. He brought out about 170 titles of Polish and foreign literature, including a three-volume selection of J. I. Kraszewski's works, with illustrations by Henryk Pillati. Natanson's books were marked by high substantive and graphic standards, and there were very few typographical errors in them. He once wrote: "My edition of *Maria* by Malczewski was without an error. I offered a gold ducat for an error, and nobody has found one!" He spared no expenses for luxurious, and thus often unprofitable, publications, and was generous to the authors. In 1868, because of his numerous occupations connected with running his own enterprises, such as the Banking House, the Insurance Company, the Mining Company, the Mirków Paper Factory, and also others in which he was a shareholder, he closed down the bookshop and sold it at half its value. Natanson was also very active in civic work: he headed the Department of Free Libraries of the Warsaw Charity Society, was a member of the Building Committee and later chairman of the High Synagogue in Tłomackie Street.

His son (or maybe a nephew he had brought up), Bronisław (1865—1906), a lawyer, civic leader and publisher, strove to "bring about an upheaval in the muddled and speculative publishing relations". Unable, on account of "disloyalty", to secure a concession to run a publishing firm, he entered into partnership with Jan Fiszer and became a respected Polish publisher. He was renowned for the high (tenfold) honoraria he paid to the authors, among them Władysław Reymont, who at Natanson's request began writing *The Peasants*, to Stefan Żeromski for *Homeless People*, to Eliza Orzeszkowa, and to many others. On the centenary of Adam Mickiewicz's birth, he brought out *A Memorial Book*. He also published many works in the field of philosophy, history, natural and social sciences, and the then popular works of H. G. Wells. In 1900, on account of bad health, Natanson closed down both the publishing firm and the bookshop. For many years, he financially supported free libraries, which would later enrich the collection of the Public Library in Koszykowa Street.

The career of the publisher Józef Unger (1817—74) was unusual. He was the son of poor parents, who, however, saw to it that he receive a good education. He attended the Piarist school and later the rabbinical school in Warsaw. He learnt the printing trade at a printing office founded by Warsaw University professors and run by A. Gałęzowski. He bought his own firm at a bargain price. It was a small, run-down printing office, of which he was for some time the sole employee. Thanks to his talent and strenuous efforts, the firm soon began to prosper, becoming one of the largest in the country. His typographical works had its own type foundry, wood-engraving studio, and binding plant. It printed newspapers and magazines, including *Dziennik Warszawski, Izraelita, Szkice i Obrazki, Tygodnik Ilustrowany,* of which Unger was the publisher, and *Wędrowiec.* He deserved credit for the development of wood-engraving techniques. Collaborating with the firm were such excellent artists as Juliusz Kossak, Henryk Pillati, and Franciszek Kostrzewski. Unger also published a hundred-odd titles of books, among them works by Józef Ignacy Kraszewski, Deotyma, Henryk Rzewuski, poetry by Władysław Syrokomla, religious books, manuals, and music scores. Greatly popular were — published from 1846 — *The Warsaw Popular Science Calendars.* Unger was an active man. He was an elder in the Warsaw Printers' Assembly; he ran a gallery of paintings by contemporary Polish painters; he was a collector of paintings by Jewish artists, among them Edmund Perl and Stanisław Heiman. After Unger's death, his firm was taken over by his adopted son Gracjan.

The popular Warsaw printers and booksellers included Salomon (later Franciszek Salezy) Lewental (1841—1902), the son of Dawid, a teacher, philosopher, and writer. A graduate of the Warsaw rabbinical school, Lewental began his publishing career as an apprentice in the firm of his future father-in-law, Jan Glücksberg. After the latter's death, he took over the enterprise and in time considerably developed it. His most popular publications included the *Popular Calendar,* brought out in 15,000 copies — a record by contemporary standards. Lewental made a particular contribution in the field of periodicals. He was the publisher of *Kłosy, Tygodnik Romansów i Powieści, Świt,* and in 1887 he bought half of the shares of Warsaw's largest daily *Kurier Warszawski.* In 1873, he commenced the publication of a huge series entitled Library of the Best Works of European Literature, within which there appeared works by T. T. Jeż, Józef Korzeniowski, Józef Ignacy Kraszewski, Eliza Orzeszkowa, Michał Bałucki, Aleksander Fredro as well as by Byron, Calderón, Goethe, Lermontov, Stendhal, Homer, Sophocles, and many others. All in all, he published 285 titles. He was a respected philantropist, for a dozen or more years a member of the Jewish Community, one of the initiators of building the Synagogue in Tłomackie Street. He was also the founder of free clinics for the poor in Warsaw hospitals.

Another popular Warsaw bookseller was Marian Sztajnsberg (b. 1887, d. 1943 in the Warsaw ghetto), co-owner, together with Stanisław and Tadeusz Markusfeld, of the firm Ferdynand Hoesick Booksellers, Co. Ltd. He was, in the first place, the publisher of legal literature, including 81 volumes (until 1934) of *Hoesick Texts of Laws in Force in the Polish Republic.* During the Nazi occupation, Sztajnsberg could be encountered selling books in Leszno Street, in the ghetto territory.

A popular figure in music circles was Józef Kaufman, the owner of a music score storehouse and lending library in Warsaw and of well-supplied bookshop.

Of the Jewish publishers, printers, and booksellers of the late 19th and the early 20th centuries, at least a few more deserve mention. They include Gabriel Centnerszwer (1841—1917), a teacher's son and graduate of the Warsaw rabbinical school, who ran a well-stocked bookshop in Marszałkowska Street. Herman Altenberg (1848—85), who, together with Maurycy Robitschek, ran a bookshop and a painting storehouse, was a merited publisher of reproductions of works by Polish painters. Having moved to Warsaw from Lvov, where he had been born, Altenberg opened a bookshop and a lending library. He was also the publisher of the Library of Polish Classics and the Library of Amateur Theatres. Another well-known bookseller and publisher was Teodor Paprocki (1857—95), who, in partnership with Władysław Dłużniewski, kept a bookshop T. Paprocki and Co. in Chmielna Street in Warsaw. He published works of literature, philosophy, history, the exact sciences, technology as well as a belles-lettres series, and a Library of Romances and Novels.

Mention should also be made of the Cracow printer and publisher, Jakub Mendel Himmelblau, and his successors. Himmelblau founded his bookshop in the middle of the 19th century. In 1863, he published a book *Evenings Under the Linden,* subtitled *A History of the Polish Nation.* He also brought out Lucjan Tomasz Rycharski's textbook *A Historical Critical Outline of Polish Literature.* One of his sons, Fabian, carried on his bookselling and publishing activity and brought out a number of valuable books, including Stanisław Koźmian's *Theatrical Matters* (1904), Teofil Lenartowicz's poetry (1876), a study on Wincenty Pol by Lucjan Siemieński as well as many books for young people, among them *Robinson Crusoe* and the books by J.F. Cooper.

One of Jakub Himmelblau's daughters married Henryk Frist, who at first ran a shop selling writing utensils and picture frames. He soon became Cracow's chief seller of post-cards and, eventually, the owner of a Polish Painters' Salon, where he sold paintings by the Kossaks, Malczewski, Fałat, Stachiewicz, Axentowicz, and many others, from whom he purchased the exclusive rights to reproduction. After the First World War the firm was expanded by Henryk's brothers, Julian and Józef, both holding doctor's degrees in law. They founded the Akropol printing works, which employed such modern techniques as offset and lithography. Theirs was the only firm in interwar Poland making reproductions of paintings which matched the world's highest standards.

The picture of the Jewish printers' and publishers' community in Cracow would be incomplete without mentioning Napoleon (Naphtali) Telz (1866—1943), a printer and publisher and, from 1897, the owner of the Cracow National Printing House, which among other things published daily newspapers such as *Dziennik Poranny* and later *Dziennik Krakowski, Naprzód* (the official journal of the Polish Socialist Party), as well as numerous magazines. Telz specialized in the field of belles-lettres, bringing out the works of Seweryn Goszczyński, Adam Mickiewicz, Juliusz Słowacki, Jan Kasprowicz, Władysław Orkan, Lucjan Rydel, Stefan Żeromski, Kazimierz Przerwa-Tetmajer, and many others. He also published *The Jewish War* by Josephus Flavius, a number of socio-political works, including books by Bolesław Limanowski and Stanisław Mendelson, as well as artistic literature, e. g. Feliks Kopera's *History of Painting in Poland*, and, last but not least, the first edition of Marian Falski's *Primer.* By 1935, the National Printing House had brought out a total of 3,118 titles. For his publications, adorned with fine ornaments and illustrations (by, among others, Leon Wyczółkowski and Władysław Konieczny), Telz received many awards and medals in Poland and abroad. He chaired the Union of Printing Office Proprietors in Western Galicia and the Corporation of Typographical Industrialists in Cracow, and was active on the Central Board of the Organization of Typographical Unions in Warsaw. During the Second World War, Telz, like all Jews, had to go into hiding and died in the Warsaw ghetto. The National Printing House has functioned till this day, under state management.

Of course, those mentioned above were not the only Jewish publishers and booksellers in Cracow. The list also includes the Seidens, the Taffets, the Rauchers, the Wertheims, the Litmans, and many others. All of them made a fine contribution to the development of Polish culture.

A few words are due to the Jewish publishers and booksellers of the interwar period, who carried on the good traditions of their predecessors.

One of the more popular publishing and bookselling establishments in Warsaw was the firm of Jakub Mortkowicz (1876—1931). Having taken over, in 1912, Gabriel Centnerszwer's bookshop,

Mortkowicz founded, together with Teodor Teoplitz, a firm J. Mortkowicz Publishing Company in Warsaw. His well-provided bookshop at 12 Mazowiecka Street, run like a club, attracted Warsaw's cultural and literary élite. The patrons included Miriam, Bolesław Leśmian, Janusz Korczak, Stefan Żeromski, Maria Dąbrowska, Maria Kuncewiczowa, to mention but a few. Mortkowicz, who trade-marked his publications with the design of a corn-ear and the letters JM, specialized in belles-lettres. He was the exclusive publisher of Żeromski's books and brought out many works by Maria Dąbro-wska, Wacław Berent, Janusz Korczak, and Maria Kuncewiczowa, the poetry of the Skamander group (the series Under the Sign of Poets), a series of Polish and foreign writers, albums e.g. *History of Art in Poland*). All in all, he had published about 700 titles by 1931. Mortkowicz was a co-found-er of the Polish Book House and the Ruch Railway Bookshops, an active member of the Polish Publishers' Society and the Union of Booksellers. He was decorated with the Officer's Cross of the Polonia Restituta Order. After his death, the publishing firm and bookshop were run by his wife Ja-nina, née Horwitz (1875—1960).

Jakub Przeworski (1875—1935) was another popular Warsaw bookseller and publisher, although he operated on a smaller scale. As the well-known bibliophile, Jan Michalski (1876—1950), recalls, Przeworski "... was married — as is customary among the Jews — very young and rented, for the meagre dowry, a small shop in Świętokrzyska Street, later so well known to numerous collectors..." His training at A. H. Kleinsinger's second-hand bookshop taught him to feel the value of books — even of unmarketable books which he often bought dirt-cheap and stored in his bookshop. Before the First World War, he smuggled Warsaw publications across the border to Lvov, Cracow, and Poznań — and in the opposite direction prohibited publications to Warsaw. In 1933, he moved his bookshop to 2 Sienkiewicz Street, where he expanded his business and commenced publishing activity. He brought out chiefly translations, but also Polish literature. His vigorous activity was interrupted by his death, but the enterprise was taken over by his son Marek (1903—43), a graduate of Warsaw Technical University. Altogether, by 1939 the Przeworski firm had brought out over 300 titles, very carefully edited and exquisitely designed, among them *A History of Polish Culture* edited by Aleksander Brückner, *My Żyrardów* by Paweł Hulka-Laskowski, the poetry and children's books of Julian Tuwim, poems by Antoni Słonimski, Kazimierz Wierzyński and Homer. In December 1939, the Przeworski firm was taken over by the Nazi administrator, Paul Kostrzewa. Marek Prze-worski was put in the Warsaw ghetto whence he escaped, but soon he was shot by the Gestapo.

The victims of the Warsaw ghetto included Michał Fruchtman. Before the war, he was frequently persecuted by the authorities for his leftist convictions and contacts with the Communist Party of Poland, for which he illicitly printed brochures. He ran his bookshop in Świętokrzyska Street in part-nership with his son. He commenced publishing activity in 1927 and brought out books by progres-sive authors, among them Wacław Rogowicz, Halina Krahelska, Antonina Sokolicz as well as the works of Egon Erwin Kisch and Karol Radek.

Another Jewish publisher who died in the Warsaw ghetto was Henryk Lindenfeld, until 1912 J. Mortkowicz's partner. His ambition was to bring out scientific works. He published, inter alia, *Darwinism and Contemporary Knowledge,* with an introduction by Ludwik Krzywicki.

Many of those mentioned were true lovers of books and experts in their field. To them, the book was not merely an object of trade, but the aim of life, an incessant fascination. One of such people was Jankiel Gutstadt, the first and, for many years, only bookseller in Łódź, who founded his book-shop in 1848. Mention is also due to second-hand booksellers — great collectors and booksellers in the best meaning of the word. Significantly, many Jewish booksellers and publishers commenced their careers as proprietors of second-hand bookshops.

Until the Second World War, Świętokrzyska Street in Warsaw was the centre of Jewish trade in second-hand books. Jewish second-hand bookshops could also be found in Elektoralna, Krucza, Marszałkowska, Nalewki, Gęsia, and other streets. Most of them were closed on Saturdays, as their proprietors were in large part orthodox Jews.

The regular customers of those bookshops included expert bibliophiles who, rummaging through the piles of jumbled books, at times would find priceless rarities which only they could appreciate.

The most eminent among Jewish second-hand book dealers was the Zalcstein family, the progenitor of which, Gecel Zalcstein (1773—1841), the son of a wealthy Nuremberg merchant, refused to take over his father's enterprise and engaged in the book trade. He began with purchasing old books. As he could not afford to open a bookshop, he stood in Długa or Miodowa Street with a basket full of volumes. Having earned some money, he moved his business to his home in Mariensztat, where outstanding writers, scholars, and students would visit him for almost half a century. The Jewish historian, Henryk Kroszczor, wrote of him: "Two large libraries of great scientific importance and national value were created thanks to the expert aid of Zalcstein. One of them was the later priceless Library of the Krasiński Estate. ... In order to buy the resources for the library, Zalcstein visited manors and purchased rare judaica, incunabula, exquisite prints from the period of the Renaissance and the Reformation..."

Religious books were an important field of Jewish publishing activity in Poland. Prayer-books, the Bible, the books of the Talmud and theological treatises were printed by specialized printing offices. The printing process was very difficult; the composition required the use of types of varying face and size. The small printing offices produced original and expensive editions of religious works which were in great demand.

Another important line of Jewish printing, publishing, and bookselling was Jewish literature in Yiddish. Such books were printed by the well-equipped press printing works and sold by specialized Jewish bookshops, of which Warsaw had over twenty. They were published, on the principles of subscription, by civic, political, and cultural organizations, such as the Kultur-Liga associated with the Jewish organization Bund. At times, a partnership was formed to publish the collected works of some prominent Jewish writer, as was the case with the publication of the works of Mendele Mokher Sefrim. The leading Warsaw Jewish newspapers rewarded their regular subscribers with classics of Jewish literature.

LITERATURE

No other nation uses the word "literature" in so many meanings as the Jews do. This concerns, above all, the language. The Jews wrote and write either in Hebrew ('ibrît), or in Jewish (Yiddish), or in the language of the country in which they lived or are living.

The Polish territories had played a special part in the development of Jewish literature. For it was there that many of the trends of classical Jewish literature originated, spreading next to other countries of the Diaspora.

Let us devote some attention to secular Jewish literature, dividing it into literature written in Hebrew and literature in Yiddish. Let us also note the role of Jews in Polish literature.

Until the end of the 18th century. Hebrew literature included mainly Talmudic works. It originated in Eastern Europe, which, in this respect, held a central position in the world. From the end of the 18th century onwards, because of contacts with Western culture, Modern Hebraic literature came into being. It can be divided into two epochs, as it were: the enlightenment, or *Haskalah,* and the renaissance, or *Sifrut hat'chiya.* The dividing line between these two epochs is, of course, a matter of convention, since interest in secular culture and some trends proper to the *Haskalah* appeared when rabbinical literature was still in full flower. The *Haskalah*, which had originated among the disciples of the Berlin philosopher, Moses Mendelssohn, reached Poland in the early 19th century thanks to several Jewish scholars and writers and developed, in particular, in Galicia, Volhynia, and the Vilna region. Noteworthy among the representatives of this trend are such Hebrew authors as Mendel Lewin of Satanów (1750—1823); Joseph Perl (1770—1840); Nachman Krochmal (1785—1840); Solomon Judah Rappaport (1790—1878); Isaac Erter (1794—1851), the author of colourful, satirical descriptions of the life of Jews in Galicia; Meir Letteris, Krochmal's disciple, a poet and translator of the works of Schiller, Byron, and Racine; and Samuel Leib Goldenberg of Tarnopol, the founder of the journal *Kerem Hemed* which appeared in the years 1833 to 1843.

The Russian partition zone, like the Austrian, also witnessed the development of Hebrew literature and the attendant enlightenment movement, aimed, above all, at ensuring education to the mass of people. A prominent role in the movement was played by Isaac Baer Levinsohn (1788—1860). He wrote philosophical treatises, poems, satire as well as polemics refuting insinuations against the Jews and their faith (he demonstrated, inter alia, that ritual murder charges were nonsensical). The early period of the *Haskalah* also witnessed the activity of Mordecai Aaron Guenzberg (1796—1847), a popularizer of knowledge, the author of works on the discovery of America, the history of Russia as well as of descriptions of travels, tales, and dramatized letters. Abraham Dov Lebensohn (1794—1879), an instructor of Hebrew and Armaic at the Vilna rabbinical school, is regarded as a leading representative of the enlightenment. He wrote biblical treatises, but was best known as the author of dramas aimed against orthodox fanatics.

Of the younger representatives of the Jewish enlightenment, mention is due to Joshua Heschel Schorr (1812—92), called "a Galician Voltaire"; Fabius Mieses (1834—93), the author of translations from Latin literature (*Sire Romi*); and Nathan Samuely (1846—1921), a poet, the author of short stories about the life of Galician Jews. Moreover, a group of popularizers of science was active at that time, led by Hayyim Selig Słonimski (1840—1904), the author of such treatises as *Mosedei Hokhmah* (Bases of Wisdom), *Kokhva de-Shavit* (Comet), and *Toledot ha-Shamayim* (The History of the Skies).

Many Hebrew writers lived in Vilna, among them Micah Joseph Lebensohn (1828—52), the author of biblical poems whose main characters are King Solomon, Samson, and the dying Moses. The life of King David was described by the excellent poet, Leon Gordon (1830—92). His work was influenced by Abraham Mapu (1808—66), a Hebrew writer from Kovno. Of great importance for the development of Hebrew literature was the monthly *Ha-Shahar* (The Dawn, 1868—85), founded by the writer and publicist Perez Smolenskin (1842—85). The monthly, regarded as the central Hebrew literary journal, published, among other things, the works of Mordecai David Brandstaedtter (1844—1926), the precursor of the Hebrew short story, the author of humorous stories showing the life of Jews in small towns. The contributors of the *Ha-Shahar* included Leon Gordon. Another Hebrew literary journal was *Ha-Boker* (The Morning), published by the poet Abraham Baer Gotlober (1811—99).

In the late 19th century, some Hebrew writers sympathized with the ideas of socialism. They included Isaac Kaminer (1834—1901), Judah Loeh Levin (1845—1926), and Ben Nec (or, properly: Benzion Novakhovichi, 1856—1931). They published their works in the Hebrew socialist journal *Ha-emet* (The Truth) which appeared in Vienna. There were also supporters of the national-conservative movement, represented, among others, by Yehiel Michael Pines (1844—1913) and Ze'ev Jawitz (1847—1924), the author of *The Great History of the Jews* (9 volumes had been published by 1936).

At the turn of the 19th century, a trend called the renaissance made its appearance. Its representatives included such talented writers and poets as Nahum Sokolow (1860—1936), a historian, novelist, poet, literary critic, and translator (he translated from Polish Alexander Kraushar's work *Frank and the Frankists*); Abraham Shalom Friedberg (1893—1902), one of the leaders of the Zionist movement; and first of all, David Frischmann (1860—1922), editor of Hebrew journals, writer, publicist, poet, and translator who rendered into Hebrew the masterpieces of Shakespeare, Goethe, Byron, Ibsen, Nietsche, and Tagore. Frischmann held a critical attitude toward the *Haskalah* and is thought to have put Hebrew literature onto a modern track. Hebrew was also the language of the first works of the two most outstanding Jewish writers: Isaac Leib Peretz and Shalom Jacob Abramovitsch. The latter was later to write in Yiddish under the pen-name of Mendele Mokher Sefarim (Mendele, the Itinerant Bookseller).

A sizeable group of authors writing in Hebrew appeared in the early 20th century. The most prominent of them included Hayyim Nahman Bialik (1873—1934), Itzhak Katzenelson (1886—1944), Isaiah Bershadsky (1870—1908), Hillel Zeitlin (1871—1942), Uri Zvi Gniesin (1880—1913), and Micha Josef Berdyczewski (1865—1921). Only few of this group wrote novels and short stories — and did this rather rarely. The one exception was Joseph Opatoshu (properly: Opatowski, 1887—1954), who wrote chiefly in Yiddish. He was, however, the author of an excellent book in Hebrew, *Be-ya'arot Polin* (In Polish Woods), which was rendered into Yiddish and Polish and was filmed in Warsaw before the war. Opatoshu also wrote the novel *The Year 1863*, with a subtitle *The Jews Are Fighting for Poland's Independence*, which was rendered into Polish.

Mattityahu Moshe Polakevich (1893—1937), who wrote under the pen-name Mattityahu Moshe Shoham, was one of the most outstanding representatives of Hebrew-language literature in the interwar period. In his lyrics written in rhyme, blank verse, or prose, he tackled philosophical and moral problems. He was also a precursor of Hebraic dramaturgy. His dramas, full of bathos, written in an archaizing style, like *Yeriho* (Jericho), *Bilam* (Balaam), *Zor vi-Yrushalyim* (Tyre and Jerusalem), *Elohei Barzel...* (Thou Shalt not make to thyself molten gods), in spite of their biblical themes, contained many allusions to contemporaneity. He was, moreover, a teacher of Modern Hebraic literature at Warsaw's Institute of Judaic Sciences, chairman of the Union of Hebrew Writers, and president of the Hebrew PEN-Club in Warsaw.

Aside from belles-lettres, the Hebrew language served as a medium for many scientific works, such as Ezriel Nathan Frenk's *Ha-Ironim ve-ha-Yehudim be-Polin* (Burghers and Jews in Poland), *Yehudei Polin bi-Ymei Milhamot Napoleon* (Jews of Poland in the Time of Napoleon) and *Letoldot ha Yehudin ba-nesichut Warsha* (On the History of Jews in the Duchy of Warsaw). Many valuable treatises dealing with Polish Jews were also written by Meir Balaban.

The picture of Hebrew literature would be incomplete if we did not mention Hebraic translations from Polish literature. The first Polish poet to have been translated into Hebrew was Adam Mickiewicz. In 1842, the twelve-year-old Judah, later Julian, Klaczko translated *Faris* and somewhat later *Daddy's Return*. *Faris* had several other translators, including M. Z. Lebenson, Ch. J. Borensztajn, and J. Lichtenbaum. Several of Mickiewicz's poems, including the *Nymph of Lake Świteź*, were translated by Aaron Zeitlin. In 1881, Mojżesz Jechiel Ascorielli superbly rendered into Hebrew *Books of the Polish Nation and of the Polish Pilgrimage*, the rendition having been introduced by Mickiewicz's friend, Arnaud Lèvy. The above mentioned Lichtenbaum translated three of the books of *Pan Thaddeus.* He also rendered into Hebrew poems by Juliusz Słowacki and Maria Konopnicka. Zygmunt Krasiński's *Iridion* was translated by Hayyim Ben-Abraham, Stanisław Wyspiański's *Anathema* by A. Zeitlin, and H. Sienkiewicz's *Trilogy* by E. N. Frenk and A. Lewinson. Numerous short stories, some of them comprised in *An Anthology of Polish Short Stories*, were translated by Jehuda Warszawiak. Among them were stories by Orzeszkowa, Konopnicka, Prus, Reymont, Sienkiewicz, and Żeromski. Also translated were *My First Battles* by Józef Piłsudski and *Marshal Józef Piłsudski* by Wacław Sieroszewski. An immense interest was aroused by the Hebrew edition of Władysław Reymont's *The Peasants*, translated by Hayyim Ben-Abraham and published in Tel-Aviv by the firm of A. J. Shtibl, a Jew from Poland who ardently promoted Polish literature in Hebrew translations. The latter also brought out Sienkiewicz's *Quo Vadis* and *In Desert and Wilderness.* Most of the authors of Hebrew translations of Polish literature appearing abroad — first in Palestine and after the war in Israel — have been Jews from Poland. Among the poets whose works have been translated into Hebrew, one can find such names as Jan Kochanowski, Leopold Staff, Bolesław Leśmian, Jarosław Iwaszkiewicz, Julian Tuwim, Kazimierz Wierzyński, Józef Wittlin, Antoni Słonimski, and many others. Also translated were some Polish dramas, including Jerzy Żuławski's *End of the Messiah* and Zofia Nałkowska's *The Day of His Return*, both of which were staged by the Hebrew theatre Habima.

Hebrew-language literature could not exert a strong influence, since the mass of the Jewish people knew that language rather poorly — chiefly for religious purposes. Hebrew was, first and foremost, the language of the Jewish intellectual élite. Hence, in the last quarter of the 19th century, there appeared numerous authors writing in Yiddish. An example of this change are the afore-mentioned Peretz and Abramovitsch, who went down in the history of literature — not only of Jewish literature, as they were widely translated — precisely as authors writing in Yiddish. It was thanks to them that the modern Yiddish language began to take shape.

Thus the late 19th century witnessed the inception and success of Yiddish-language literature.

The Jewish writers had not missed the chance offered by a widely understood language. They became intimate and loved, popular and famous, and some of them really deserve being called great. It was thanks to them that Poland, which for centuries had been the cradle of great Jewish intellectual movements, also became the cradle of Yiddish-language literature. Some Jewish writers, even those who had emigrated from Poland e.g. to the United States, like Sholem Asch, Abraham Reisen, Joseph Opatoshu, and others, would not sever their links with Polish Jewry, both in terms of the themes and the colour of their works.

The leading Jewish literary classics included Mendele Mokher Sefarim (Shalom Jacob Abramovitsch, 1836—1917), Isaac Leib Peretz (1851—1915), Shalom Aleichem (Solomon Rabinowitz, 1859—1916), and Sholem Asch (1880—1957)

I. L. Peretz was doubtless the most prominent of the four. Born at Zamość, he was the offspring of a Sephardic family brought into Poland by Jan Zamoyski toward the end of the 16th century. He was a self-taught man who had acquired profound knowledge in the domain of history, philosophy, law, sociology, and the natural sciences. He had a command of several foreign languages. In 1876, he obtained a licence to establish a law firm in Zamość. He was the legal adviser of the Zamoyski Estate and a defender of the rights of people persecuted by tsarism. Peretz's stay in Zamość had strongly influenced his personality. Sensitive to the beauty of nature and keenly interested in Jewish and Polish legends and local customs, deeply concerned about the sad life of the small-town poor, Peretz had become a writer strongly attached to the community and the region he came from. His rich literary output includes poetry and prose as well as journalism. He combined the romantic fantasy with an observation of life. He started writing in Hebrew — chiefly poems not devoid of social accents, e.g. *Bait shome'm* (The Deserted House), *Ha-azel* (Lazybones), *Hair ha-katan* (A Small Town), *Li Omerim* (They Tell Me...). He also wrote in Polish — for example, a collection of his works in manuscript form entitled *Poems with Various Contents* has been preserved.

Peretz's great talent manifested itself in his first works in Yiddish, i. a. *Zamoshcher podzondkes* (The State of Affairs in Zamość), a bitter satire upon the local Jewish community, or the poem *Monish*, dealing with a Jewish boy's love for a beautiful Christian girl. The latter poem commenced the romantic trend in Jewish poetry. Many of Peretz's works contained distinct social accents.

In 1888, Peretz moved to Warsaw, whence he frequently travelled to small towns in the Tomaszów Mazowiecki county. The fruit of these travels was a series of short stories collected in the volume *Bilder fun a Provints-Rayze* (Pictures from a Provincial Journey). The plot of most of these stories, including *Inem postwagen* (In the Stage Coach), *Meshulekh* (Messenger), *Sholem Bays* (Idyll), *Emes un shek* (Truth and Lie), *Boshragg* (Bończek the Silent Beggar), or *Di frame kats* (The Devout Cat), is set in small, dingy towns. Peretz's stories are remarkable for their beautiful language and warm, though sarcastic, humour.

The neo-romantic trend in Jewish literature was initiated by Peretz's two series of stories which were the top achievements of his literary output: *Khasidish* (Hasidic Motifs) and *Folkstimlikhe geshikhten* (Folk Tales), brought out in 1889—1904.

Peretz was also an outstanding playwright who remained under the influence of Ibsen and Wyspiański. His best known dramas include: *Di Goldene keyt* (The Golden Chain), *In polish oyf der Keyt* (Chained in the Vestibule), *Baynakht oyfn Altn Mark* (At Night in the Old Market), and the comedy *Amol iz gewen a meylakh* (There Was a King...).

Peretz's works were translated into many European languages, and even into Esperanto. In Poland, they appeared in almost all Jewish and Polish magazines and in a number of collections. The first collection of his short stories in Polish was published in 1898 and another one in 1925. In 1958, *A Selection of Stories* by I.L. Peretz appeared within the National Library series. He died and was buried in Warsaw, and his funeral was attended by over a hundred thousand persons, including prominent representatives of Polish literature.

We will omit the afore-mentioned, outstanding classic of Jewish literature, Mendele Mokher Sefarim (Shalom Jacob Abramovitsch), as his works, after he had moved to Odessa, were only loosely connected with Polish themes. Nonetheless, he was very popular in Poland, where his novels were published — and some of them translated into Polish. including *The Jewish Don Quixote* (transl. by K.J. Szaniawski 1869) and *The Jade* (1886).

Similarly, it might appear that neither should Shalom Aleichem be regarded as a representative of Polish Jewish literature. That great writer, however — ranked next to Gogol, Dickens, and Mark Twain, a friend of Gorky's, a distinguished humanist, who was said to be the greatest Jewish humorist and tragedian at the same time — showed us in his works a captivating, sorrowful but also hopeful, picture of the small Jewish town of the late 19th century. The Polish Jews thought him to be their own writer. He was linked with Poland by numerous ties. He travelled to Warsaw and Łódź, Vilna and Baranowicze where, infirmed by a grave, incurable disease, he died surrounded with the sympathy of the local population, Jews and Poles alike. He was, next to Peretz, one of the most widely read Jewish writers. All his works were published several times in Poland, and many of them were rendered into Polish. *Menakhem Mendl* appeared in 1904, translated by Jerzy Or, and *The Notes of a Commercial Traveller* in 1923, reissued in 1958 with an introduction by Jarosław Iwaszkiewicz. Other translations of his works included: *Stempenyu,* a collection of humorous stories, *The En-*

chanted Tailor, Motel, the Cantor's Son, The Story of Tevye the Dairyman, and *Marienbad.* Shalom Aleichem (the pseudonym means "Peace be unto you") is also the author of a drama *Tsezeyt un Tsershprey* (Scattered and Dispersed). His last work was an autobiographical novel entitled *Back from the Fair* (from the fair of his own life), in which bitter irony mixed with the sad reality.

Sholem Asch is regarded as a continuator, as it were, of Peretz's literary style. He, too, described with an epic verve the life of his compatriots against the background of various historical situations. His works, imbued with faith in man and filled with optimism as well as marked by a profound knowledge of the Jewish community, evince love for the people. His strong, human ties with the tormented nation could be discerned in his last works, written during the Second World War, which he spent in America, where he had lived for several score years. At times, his works were strikingly realistic, but they did not lack romanticism and mysticism, either. Sholem Asch, though he was ideologically and stylistically linked with his predecessors, was a modern writer. His first works, written in Polish though they dealt with biblical themes, were influenced by leading Polish writers. He was a friend of Stanisław Witkiewicz and Stefan Żeromski and corresponded with Władysław Orkan, Eliza Orzeszkowa, and Bolesław Prus.

His first major book *Dos Shtetl* (The Little Town), written in 1904, won him a great popularity. It appeared in Polish in 1910. Equally well received was the volume of his short stories (1906) dedicated to Stanisław Witkiewicz. In 1914, he emigrated to the United States, where he wrote the novel *Uncle Moses and America,* dealing with Jewish emigrants. His numerous novels and short stories are firmly rooted in social and historical realities, e.g. *Die Muter* (Mother, Polish ed. 1933), *Motke ganev* (Motke the Thief), the trilogy *Farn mabul* (Before the Flood, 1929, 1930, translated into English as *Three Cities,* Polish ed. 1930—1931). After the second World War, he wrote an elegy *Triumphal March* (published in Polish in the monthly *Odra,* 1958), devoted to the Polish Jews murdered by the Nazis.

Asch is also the author of several dramas. The tragedy *Got fun Nekomeh* (God of Vengeance, 1907) was played in many languages and on many stages of the world. His well-known dramas also include *Sabbatai Zvi,* about a false Messiah, and *A Union of Weaklings.* His dramaturgy has contributed to the development of the Jewish theatre.

Hersh David Nomberg (1876—1927) was contemporary of Asch. Albeit his works were strongly influenced by Peretz, the world of his characters was not confined to the old, but also embraced the contemporary Jewish milieux. It was precisely on Peretz's advice that Nomberg quit writing in Hebrew and switched into Yiddish.

He initially published his works in the journals of Warsaw, Vilna and Cracow. He was a novelist, short story writer, essayist, and publicist. His first works critically showed the old, traditional Jewish world. Though fascinated by progress, science, and the young intelligentsia, he felt close to poor, lonely, lost people who most often were the heroes of his novels. Nomberg's most popular books include: *Der Figelman* (Bird of Heaven). *Di Kursistke* (The Student), *A shpil in libe* (Love Play), and *In poylisher Yeshiwah* (In a Polish Yeshiva). He also wrote stories dealing with the life of children. He was highly praised for his translations into Yiddish of Shakespeare, Hauptmann, Tagore. His works, published in various journals, including Polish-language ones, several times appeared in the form of collections. His drama *Di Mishpokhe* (The Family), which depicts the demoralization of an ancient Hasidic family, was played in many Jewish theatres, and the author was highly valued by the Polish literary community. His funeral was attended by a delegation of the Polish Writers' Union, including Leopold Staff, Jan Lechoń, and Ferdynand Goetel.

Joshua Perle (1888—1943) in his novel *Yidn fun a gants Yor* (Everyday Jews), depicted the life of Jews in small towns over half a century. The novel won him an award funded by the socialist Bund and the Peretz award. Isaac Meir Weissenberg (1881—1938) devoted most of his works to the ordinary man, although his picture of the life of Jews in a small town is less idyllic; he gives a more drastic description of their hopeless life and poverty. Simon Horontchik (1889—1939), in his novel *Geroysh fun Mashinen* (Whirr of Machines), pays much attention to the life of workers, going into the intimate aspect of this life. Efraim Kaganowski (1893—1958), on the other hand, has imbued his works with serenity, wisdom, and humour. It is not without reason that he is being compared to Maupassant and Chekhov. In the profoundly psychological prose and poetry of Zusman Segalowitch (1884—1949), there prevail such age-old human problems as love and hatred, faithfulness and deceit. Israel Joshua Singer (1893—1944), a master of popular novels, was the author of a once popular book *Yoshe Kalb,* a satire on the life of Hasidim and *Di Brider Ashkenazi* (The Ashkenazi Brothers), a saga on Łódź financial circles. Both novels, adapted for the stage by Maurice Schwartz, were played in Jewish theatres. The novels of Joseph Opatoshu devote much attention to the Jews' participation in the struggle for Poland's independence, notably their participation in the January 1863 Insurrection. Many Jewish writers lived in Poland before the Second World War. Some of them had emigrated before the war, others the turmoil of war had scattered all over the world. Most of those who survived remained faithful to the atmosphere of their youth, to the best traditions of Jewish literary classics. One example is Isaac Bashevis Singer, a Nobel Prize winner, born at Radzymin near Warsaw.

In addition, there was a large group of Jewish poets living in Poland. Itzik Manger (1901—69), the author of original folk ballads, was regarded as the most outstanding Jewish poet of the interwar period. Mention is also due to Melech Ravitch (b. 1893) who was at the same time a well-known prose writer, and Kalman Lis, the author of a poem on social themes *Dos lid fun Peter Batrak* (Peter Batrak's Song) and of excellent poems for children as well as the translator of Pushkin.

Whereas the specific Hebrew and Yiddish literature on the whole remained outside the Polish national culture, a considerable number of Jews or Poles of Jewish descent made an indisputable contribution to Polish literature. Among the latter, there was a large group of entirely Polonized Jews, whom other Jews used to call "assimilators" and who voluntarily, sometimes even at the cost of a change of religion, entered into the Polish community and Polish national culture. One of the first ones was the excellent stylist Julian Klaczko (1825—1906), in his youth the author of Hebrew poems and later an eminent literary critic, the author of works on Zygmunt Krasiński, Adam Mickiewicz, and of many literary essays and treatises.

In the mid-19th century, a circle of assimilated Jewish youths was formed in Warsaw, comprising, among others, Alexander Kraushar (1842—1931), a participant of the January 1863 Insurrection, historian, the author of a two-volume *History of Jews in Poland*, a monograph, *Colonel Berek's Son,* and of a seminal work, *The Diplomatic Calendar,* dealing with Jews in ancient Poland; Michał Mutermilch, the author of *An Outline of the History of Art* and a work on Wacław Sieroszewski; Alfred Nossig (1864—1942), a poet, the author of the libretto of Ignacy Paderewski's opera *Manru* and of such dramas as *A Tragedy of Thought, King of Zion, The Expulsion of the Jews;* Michał Bałucki, the author of still popular comedies, including *Big Shots, Mr Councillor's Councillors,* and *The Open House.*

During the period of the Young Poland movement, prominence was won by Wilhelm Feldmin (1868—1919), a friend of Adam Asnyk, Stanisław Przybyszewski, and Stanisław Wyspiański. He was a noted literary critic, the author of the monumental work *Contemporary Polish Literature,* which was reprinted 8 times before the outbreak of the Second World War, and of works on Żeromski and Wyspiański; Antoni Lange (1861—1930), a translator who translated some of the master-pieces of Hebrew, Arab, and Persian literature into Polish; Zygmunt Bromberg-Bytowski (1866—1923); Leopold Kampf (1880—1912); Arnold Szyfman (1882—1967), the founder of the Polski Theatre in Warsaw and the author of several comedies, including *Pankracy August I* and *Fifi*; Andrzej Baumfeld (pseudonym Andrzej Boleski); Józef Kwiatek, a socialist and civic leader, the author of literary treatises, including *Słowacki's Writings with Ideological-Political Contents;* and by others, including such eminent authors as Juliusz Kleiner and Ostap Ortwin.

As regards the poets of the interwar period, one should mention such names as Julian Tuwim, Bo-lesław Leśmian, Antoni Słonimski, Józef Wittlin, Adam Ważyk, Mieczysław Jastrun, Mieczysław Braun, Włodzimierz Słobodnik, Aleksander Wat, Leopold Lewin, Anatol Stern, and many others, among them authors of vaudeville texts, such as Andrzej Włast, Marian Hemar (Hescheles), Artur Tur, Emanuel Szlechter, Jerzy Jurandot, and Stefania Grodzieńska.

In the domain of prose, for example such names as Janusz Korczak, Bruno Schulz, Bruno Wina-wer, Kazimierz Brandys, Stanisław Wygodzki, Bruno Jasieński, Julian Stryjkowski, Adolf Rudnicki, Benedykt Hertz, Michał and Roman Brandstaetter, Tadeusz Peiper, Roman Karst, Irena Krzywicka, Halina Górska, Krystyna Żywulska, Jerzy Lutowski, Leo Belmont (Leopold Blumenthal), should be mentioned.

The Jewish writers — those regarded as part of the Polish literary tradition and those who wrote in Hebrew in the Polish territories — did this out of a deep inner need and the sincere conviction that their works served the nation with which they had been linked for ages and to whom they wanted. to offer everything which gave meaning to their life.

THEATRE

The historian of the theatre, Bernard Gorin, provided his two-volume *History of the Jewish Theatre* with a subtitle Two Thousand Years of the Theatre of the Jews. There has been a long, though now outdated, controversy over this thesis, in which, one should admit, there are some grains of truth.

For it is a fact that Herod the Great, the King of Judaea, not only expanded the temple of Jeru-salem, but also had theatres built in the city. The theatres showed Greek dramas, since Judaea did not have her own theatrical plays, while the devout Judeans looked with horror and outrage at the sanc-tuaries of Melpomene alien to their creed.

The reason for the lack of dramatic works in ancient Jewish literature was the prohibition set forth in the law of Moses: "Thou shalt not make unto thee any graven image, or any likeness of any thing that is in heaven above, that is in earth beneath, or that is in the water under the earth" (Exodus, 20, 4). This religious prohibition was stricly observed and applied also to the actor's art of imitating other people .

At the turn of the 5th century, when the theatre deriving from classical culture fell silent, a quasi theatre came into being in Jewish communities scattered over large parts of Europe: the theatre of Purim, the only Jewish holiday celebrated joyfully, without a fast.

Purim-shpil — spectacles and rejoicings marking the holiday of Purim — survived in Poland for many centuries. Their dramatic plot originated from the legend contained in the biblical book of Esther, telling of Ahasuerus who "reigned, from India even onto Ethiopia, over an hundred and seven and twenty provinces", of his morose and evil governor Haman, of the beautiful Hadassah-Esther and her clever cousin Mordecai. The intrigue plotted by Haman, who "sought to destroy all the Jews", eventually turned against him. Haman was hanged on the gallows which he himself had prepared for Mordecai.

Fragments of the legend, put in the form of rhymed texts, frequently frivolous, were recited or sung by masqued youths — craftsmen's apprentices or students of rabbinical schools — in the yard (*shulhof*) in front of the synagogue. The texts, mostly very primitive, sentimental or vulgar, were at first presented in the Hebrew-Aramaic language and later exclusively in the language spoken by the people, that is Yiddish or Ladino.

This was the main source of the medieval literature connected with the holiday of Purim, which also drew on other biblical legends, such as the legend of Joseph sold to the Ismaelites, of Joseph and Potiphar, of David and Goliath. This peculiar literature survived until the middle of the 19th century. There also appeared a sort of semi-professional acting in which elements of the fair-ground theatre could be discerned. The actors of these plays were called Purim-shpiler, whose successors were the Broder singers.

In order, however, that a true Jewish theatre could come into being, something more was needed than the annual celebrations of the Purim holiday with their biblical themes, or the songs and ballads of the Broder singers. What was needed was a cultural revolution. Thus the convictions had gradually to mature and consolidate among the Jewish community that the Jew's spiritual world should not have been confined to the rules and rigours of the Talmud, that outside these bounds a different life was going on, spiritually richer and more interesting, devoid of the musty smell of yeshiva volumes and closer to his authentic needs of knowledge and curiosity about the world — not the afterworld, but the world he was living in. Such a revolution was brought by the Jewish enlightenment: the *Haskalah*.

The Haskalah writers, after the fashion of the West European Enlightenment writers, chiefly French, imparted to their writings, which took the shape of bitter moral or social pamphlets, the form of dramatic works. For many decades, these works were not staged in the Polish territories, as a Jewish theatre was non-existent there. Rarely printed, they mostly circulated in handwritten copies, passed from one person to another. This is how the readers could acquaint themselves with the comedy of Isaak Euchel (1756—1854) *Mr. Henoch, or What to Do with It,* written in the last decade of the 18th century and dealing with errors in education and with a similar play written in that period by Ahron Wolfsohn (1754—1835), entitled *Recklessness and Bigotry.* Euchel and Wolfsohn were representatives of the Berlin *Haskalah* and their works, written in Yiddish, were a source of inspiration and a model for the *Haskalah* writers in central and eastern Poland.

Among the meaningful plays that initiated the *Haskalah* dramaturgy in the Polish territories, mentions is due to *The Deceitful World,* a work attributed to Mendel Lewin (1749—1823) of Satanów, the first comedy in Yiddish; the drama of Israel Axenfeld (1797—1866) of Niemirów entitled *The First Jewish Recruit,* about Nachman who, for his love of Frymeta, went to the army "for the whole town", to serve 30 years; and to the play of Solomon Ettinger (1802—56) of Warsaw, entitled *Serkele* (a diminutive form of the name Sara).

In 1888, an outstanding representative of the *Haskalah,* Abraham Ber Gottlober (1811—99), wrote of *Serkele* and Solomon Ettinger: "In 1837, I visited Zamość on several occasions. During one of the visits, I had the feeling I had contracted cholera which was then rampant in Poland. I summoned Dr Ettinger. He came, examined me, and said: 'Why talk about cholera? You'll feel better after I've read my *Serkele* to you'. He read it to me and I, listening to *Serkele,* recovered and felt like writing in Yiddish. In 1838, I wrote a comedy *Canopy* which someone later published in Warsaw, forgetting to give the author's name". *Serkele* found its way to the stage rather unexpectedly in 1862, at the rabbinical school in Zhitomir. Hayyim Selig Słonimski was the headmaster of the school at that time. His wife, the daughter of an eminent mathematician, Abraham Stern, had brought the text of *Serkele* from Warsaw and, together with the students, prepared the performance. The play was once again staged in that year, by the students of the rabbinical school in Berdyczów.

In the second half of the 19th century, there appeared the first dramatic works written in Yiddish. Initially, however, they were strongly disapproved of by the Hasidic circles and unfavourably received by the still not numerous group of enlightened Jews in Poland. There was also the audience, who wanted to hear the Jewish word spoken on the stage in a language understandable to all and telling of problems, whether comical or melodramatic, familiar to all. Finally, one more element was needed in the live Jewish theatre: professional actors. The latter appeared before the Jewish audience in the 1870's, and the man who had succeeded in combining these three elements in a harmonious whole was Abraham Goldfaden (1840—1909), called the father of the Jewish theatre.

Who were the people whom Goldfaden, and later others, had induced to become actors?

They came from various towns and localities of the "Jewish settlement zone" of the former Russian Empire, from Romania and former Galicia. They would set out in search of jobs, offering many skills, none of which could ensure them a livelihood. They tried to eke out a living by singing in inns and ale houses. They mostly came from Brody, a once prosperous town in the former Tarnopol province, where Jews constituted 70 per cent of the population. Called Broder singers, they had introduced their own style. Their songs were most often rhymed stories sung in the style of an operatic duet. These skills would later prove very useful in the newly founded Jewish theatres. The first Goldfadenian actors also included former wedding-hosts (*badchanim*), who made a business of entertaining people during sumptuous wedding receptions, as well as dismissed shop assistants, would-be synagogue cantors, and unemployed teachers (*malammedim*).

The theatrical company set up by Goldfaden in Jassy in 1886 performed his plays in the towns of Romania and south-west Russia. Wherever it went, it aroused enthusiasm which testified to the tremendous demand for a Jewish folk theatre, and Goldfaden's theatre was such. Goldfaden was not only the director of the company, but also stage manager, actor, and, above all, the author of the plays and the composer of the songs. He wrote and staged a total of 39 plays, including *Shulamis Bar Kokhva, The Recruits, Intrigue or Dwosia the Gossip, Tsvey Kuni Lemels,* and *Shmendryk.*

Due to the growing demand for theatrical performances, new theatres soon cropped up and enjoyed no lesser popularity. The leading actor of the Goldfaden theatre, Israel Grodner, quit the company and founded his own theatre. He himself did not write plays, but he found an extremely prolific author, Joseph Lateiner (1853—1918), who in the last decade of the 19th century would become one of the leading promoters of the Jewish theatre in America. He wrote about 80 plays, including 5 operas. Another playwright, Moses Hurwitch, who collaborated with Lateiner at that time, distinguished himself by an exceptional ability to adapt for the stage outstanding works of world theatrical literature, biblical tales of interest to the Jewish audience, and stories of contemporary events. The Lateiner-Hurwitch theatre was a live theatre which also took up current social and political issues of concern to the public (*The Anti-Semite or Ideology in Romania, A Rope Around the Neck or Blind Justice,* etc.).

In Warsaw, the first attempt to create a Jewish theatre was recorded in 1837. The attempt failed as a result of the opposition of the Synagogue Superintendence, which at that time was an authority in this domain. A year later, however, a five-act drama *Moses* was staged, presented "in a language which was a mixture of German and Hebrew and was written in the Hebrew alphabet, in a dialect which is used by a large part of the German and Polish Israelites" (an extremely complicated definition of the Yiddish language). As reported by a correspondent of the Berlin newspaper *Allgemeine*

Preussische Staats Zeitung, the play was authored and directed by a Mr. Scherspirer of Vienna, who also played the main character. The play was shown three times and was warmly applauded by the audience. Significantly, information about the performance appeared in a Berlin newspaper, not to mention the fact that *Moses* had been staged in Warsaw two years before the birth of Abraham Goldfaden, the "father of the Jewish theatre", and almost 40 years before he founded the first theatre in Jassy.

The assassination in 1881 of the Tsar Alexander II of Russia, and the ensuing wave of pogroms led to the closing down of the Jewish theatres. The people connected with the theatre emigrated to other countries, mainly to America. Goldfaden emigrated there, too, but he could not boast of the successes which fell to the lot of others. New York was for many years the main centre attracting the people of the Jewish theatre. The theatres functioning there, the People's Theater, Thalia Theater, or Grand-Oriental Theater, recreated on their stages the atmosphere of small Jewish towns in the eastern borderlands of the former Polish Commonwealth, thus documenting the indissoluble ties with their native country of those who, escaping pogroms or seeking jobs, found a new home on American soil.

The authors writing for the theatre included such literary celebrities as Shalom Abramovitsch, known as Mendele Mokher Sefarim (e.g. *Taxa, Prizyv*). There appeared the first reformer of the Jewish theatre, the playwright Jacob Gordin, who adapted for the Jewish stage many theatrical classics, from Lessing and Schiller to works based on Goethe's Faust (God, Man and Devil). Of the large number of works written by Gordin, mention is due, above all, to *Freedom, Mirele Efros,* and *The Jewish King Lear.* The most renowned author, however, was Solomon Rabinovitz (1859—1916), whose literary pseudonym sounds like a brotherly greeting: Shalom Aleichem. The charm of his vaudevilles, so popular half a century ago, has now declined, but his plays, such as *Stempenyu* or, in particular, *Tevye the Dairyman,* which has been made into a popular musical titled *Fiddler on the Roof* still fascinate the audience wherever they are staged.

Also popular with Jewish audiences were the dramas of Peretz Hirschbein, who wrote, under the influence of symbolism, *Aynzame welnt* (Lonely Worlds), *Khworim blumen* (Flowers on the Graves), and *Demerung* (Twilight); he subsequently took up social themes in *Die neveyle* (Carrion), *Joel, Inteligent, Grine felder* (Green Fields), *Shmids tekhter* (Smith's Daughters), and the deeply mystical *Die puste kretshme* (An Empty Inn). Isaac Leib Peretz (1852—1935) wrote dramatic works in the convention of symbolism, to mention only *The Golden Chain* and *At Night in the Old Market.*

The problems of class inequality among the Jewish community were even more strongly accentuated by David Pinski (1872—1959). His naturalist dramas *Die mame* (Mother), *Yankl der shmid* (Jankel the Smith), *Ayzik Sheftl, The Zvi Family, Shtumer Mesiach* (A Dumb Messiah) won him the name of a Jewish Berthold Brecht.

The dramaturgic talent of Halper Leivick (his true name was Leivik Halpern) developed along different lines. A would-be rabbi expelled for atheism from a yeshiva and later sent to Siberia for his participation in the workers' revolutionary movement, Leivick was the author of such excellent plays as *Der Goylem* (Golem), *Die shmates* (Rags), and *Maharam of Rutenberg.*

Ossip Dymov (1878—1942), born in Białystok, had been a publicist before he began writing for the theatre. Family conflicts were most frequently the leading motif of his dramas, and when he tackled Jewish themes he vehemently protested against lawlessness and oppression. An example of such a drama was *Shema Israel* (Listen, Israel). His play *Nu* was staged in many languages, as was his *Bronx Express,* the performance of which, in Warsaw's Ateneum Theatre in November, 1929, was reviewed by J. Appenszlak in *Nasz Przegląd* and by Karol Irzykowski in *Robotnik.*

Dramaturgy was one of the lines of activity of the most outstanding epic writer in Jewish literature, Sholem Asch (1880—1957), a native of Kutno. His dramas *With the Stream, Sabbatai Zvi, Sinner, Motke the Thief,* and *Amnon and Tamar* were cultural events of a high rank among the Jewish communities of many towns, and his *God of Vengeance* was staged in Berlin by Max Reinhard.

The above list — incomplete, of course — of authors writing for the Jewish theatre should be concluded with the name of Solomon An-Ski (1863—1920, real name: Solomon Rappaport), the author of a Jewish workers' anthem *Di Shvue* (Oath). His drama *Between Two Worlds,* known under the title of *The Dybbuk,* is a farewell, as it were, to the old world of Jewish mysticism, put in the form of a Hassidic legend.

The attempts at creating a permanent Jewish theatre had for many years encountered the opposition of Hasidic circles as well as aversion to and contempt for Jewish culture on the part of tsarist officials.

With the passage of time the situation was gradually changing. The authorities began to tolerate the "German-Jewish" language on the stage. In 1885, Abraham Goldfaden's company performed in Warsaw. What testified to the great demand for Jewish theatrical plays was the fact that the Goldfadenian *Shulamis* had 150 performances.

Toward the end of the 19th century, Jacob Ber Gimpel opened a permanent Jewish theatre in Lvov, in which the great acting talent of Berta Kalisch was born and developed.

In the early 20th century, the Jewish theatre in the territory of the Russian partition zone started to develop vigorously. The companies of Kamiński, Kampanijec, Fischsohn, and Rafael appeared in Warsaw, those of Sandberg and Spiwakowski in Łódź, and Genfer's company in Vilna. All of them frequently toured the provinces. Their repertoire included both original Jewish plays as well as translations and adaptations of works by other authors.

In 1892, Esther Rachel Kamińska made her appearance in Warsaw's Eldorado Theatre. Kamińska, who would later found the theatre in Oboźna Street, won fame as an actress during Eldorado's performances in St. Petersburg, New York, London, and Paris, where she was acclaimed as a Jewish Eleonora Duse. By her side was growing the great talent of her daughter Ida Kamińska (1899—1978).

The Jewish theatres in Poland, chiefly those in Warsaw and Vilna, would give premières of plays or theatrical adaptations by Shalom Aleichem. The audience could also acquaint themselves with Jacob Gordin's vast repertoire, previously known only in New York, and his *Mirele Efros* was also played in Polish theatres, with Wanda Siemaszko in the title role. Warsaw became the main centre of Jewish theatrical life, and Warsaw actors and actresses reinforced theatres in other towns. Eldorado, Bagatela, Ermitage, Centralny, Nowości, and Elizeum — these are the names of only some of the Jewish theatres in Warsaw, the capital of Poland, which at that time had about 350,000 Jewish inhabitants.

Although the number of Jewish theatres and actors was increasing, their repertoire was not always satisfactory. The Jewish theatres did not receive any financial assistance. Left to their own devices, they frequently had to enhance their budgets by means of a repertoire of inferior quality. Thus they staged popular vaudevilles with easy, often wistful music. The lyrics and melody of the songs would leave the theatre together with the audience and accompany them for the long time thereafter, at home and at work. Very popular were sentimental plays, the plots of which combined romance threads with social and moral motifs. The problems depicted on the stage were familiar to the audience and often wrung tears of authentic emotion. The intellectuals and press critics were disgusted, asserting that the Jewish community was waiting for a theatre which in terms of the quality of plays and acting would match the level of an intellectually mature audience. This, however, was rarely the case with the Jewish theatre.

From the perspective of the many decades that have elapsed since then, our opinions and evaluations of the Jewish theatre differ from those of the fastidious aesthetes of the 1920's and 1930's of our century. Let us bow down before the figures of actors vanishing in the mist of antiquity, the often unknown masters of theatrical illusion, whose creations roused emotions in the hearts of cobblers, baker's apprentices, junior shop assistants, or seamstresses waiting in vain for fiancées. Whoever offered them a moment of emotion or gaiety, even by means of unrefined jokes, whoever brought an illusion of a better lot into their drab, monotonous life filled with a ruthless struggle for survival — deserves respect. We believe that, in those primitive performances, the unity of the stage and the audience was accomplished — the dream of the greatest theatre directors of the world.

There was one theatrical company whose presentations frequently aroused the greatest interest, not only in Warsaw but in every town it would perform. It was called the Vilna Company, albeit during the 27 years of its activity is was linked with Vilna only for the first four years, when it was an amateur theatre. The Vilna company, founded by Jacob Ben-Ami (1912), was remarkable for its style of acting. From the times of Goldfaden, every Jewish theatre was based, in principle, on one or two outstanding actors. The Vilna Company, however, while not relinquishing outstanding individualities, succeeded in developing a style in which every actor, his every word and movement on the stage, was an important, carefully elaborated element of the whole spectacle.

In 1921, the Vilna Company split into two groups. One of them left for Vienna, later went to Romania, and returned in 1929 again to reap laurels in Warsaw, Vilna, Cracow, and Lvov. One of its plays, Sholem Asch's *Kiddush ha-Shem,* alone had about 200 performances.

While in Vienna, the company was admired by Robert Musil, who was especially fascinated by Noe Nachbusch's interpretation, in whose voice he heard echoes of synagogue chant, and by the soulful acting of Miriam Orleska. Musil was of the opinion that the Vilna Company was one of the two best theatres in Europe at that time (the other being the Stanislavsky Theatre).

The other part of the Vilna Company, which had taken on the name of the Yiddish Art Theatre, settled in America following performances in Berlin, Amsterdam, and Antwerp.

In the pre-war *Concise Statistical Yearbook* we find that in 1936, 15 Jewish theatres functioned in Poland. Let us not forget that the Jewish theatres were not subsidized by the state or municipal authorities, that their financial situation was always difficult and frequently critical. To this number we should add several score amateur theatres. The level of many of the latter was not inferior to that of professional theatres, to mention only the Vilna Company, which had evinced its basic characteristics when it had been an amateur theatre, or the workers' group Orfeusz, which performed in Esther Rachel Kamińska's theatre in Warsaw.

The hunger for theatrical performances was a permanent phenomenon which did not give way even to physical hunger in the years of the economic crisis, when theatre-halls were by no means empty. Its consequence was a hunger for repertoire which affected all theatres in the world, but which possessed special characteristics in the Jewish theatre.

The Jewish theatre in Poland, and not only in Poland, had always faced the difficult question of whether it were to be a theatre exclusively of Jewish dramaturgy, or of world dramaturgy.

At the beginning, the Jewish theatres presented immensely popular plays imbued with folk pathos, building up the national consciousness, which attempted to show in the mirror of reality the essence of Jewishness, to recreate "the truths of life" of various Jewish milieux. The theatre of Esther Rachel Kamińska in Oboźna Street played the leading role in this respect.

The theatrical audience, their social consciousness having been awakened by the 1905 revolution, were ready to accept a repertoire dramaturgically very diversified: from sentimental Jewish plays like *Scattered and Dispersed, Meshiyahs zeytn* (The Times of the Messiah), or *Di Mishpokhe* (Family) to *Hamlet* and *The Merchant of Venice*, Viennese operettas, and burlesques. Parallel to this generally favoured repertoire, there came Peretz Hirschbein's idylls and his elegiac-sentimental *Rozhinkes mit mandlen* (Raisins with Almonds), *An Empty Inn, Green Fields,* and *The Smith's Daughters.* These productions, however, lacked a good scenography, indispensable already at that time in plays on the borderline of symbolism and naturalism. This fact was obvious to theatre-goers, who recognized the principle that theatre meant not only words spoken on the stage, but also an appropriate setting for these words.

In the repertoires of artistic theatres, such as the Vilna Company, the Zygmunt Turkow Theatre and also in the vaudeville theatres Azazel, Sambatian, and Ararat, there arose the dilemma: whether only Jewish dramatury, or world dramaturgy. This dilemma in the 1920's and 1930's was not the outcome of searching for box office successes, but of the ever growing tendencies to evolve a specific artistic profile through a different style of acting, musical setting, and scenography. In particular, the role of specific Jewish motifs in music increased. An example of finding apposite solutions in this field was an original production of *The Dybbuk* by David Hermann. Some people saw in it an attempt to accentuate the mystical element, although in fact Hermann imparted to his production the form of a naturalistic impression, without a shade of mysticism. The mystical elements in *The Dybbuk* the leading play of the Jewish theatre, were emphasized in productions by other directors, e. g. Abram Morevski in Vilna, Maurice Schwartz in New York, and Vakhtangov in Moscow.

The theatre conducted by Zygmunt Turkow and his wife, Ida Kamińska, in Warsaw succeeded in achieving equilibrium between Jewish themes and the world classical repertoire, in combining excellent acting with splendid stage design, which ensured the great value of such performances as Asch's *Motke the Thief*, Ettinger's *Serkele,* or Gogol's *The Government Inspector* and Molière's *L'Avare.*

Zygmunt Turkow's theatre brought out an important feature of the Jewish theatre: the Jewish actor felt best in a comedy, whether Jewish or non-Jewish. Comedy was his element; it was in it that he was an authentic actor.

Paradoxically as it may seem, Molière's *L'Avare* came closer to the Jewish actor's possibilities of expression than did the heroes of Asch's *God of Vengeance* or Hirschbein's *An Empty Inn*. It is hard to say today whether this phenomenon was the result of subconscious reminiscences, both in actors and the audience, of the long forgotten popular Purimshpil — which for centuries had been the sole occasion for merry-making involving both the audience and the animators of the play — or whether the need of gaiety was for both the former and the latter a consequence of the conditions in which their uneasy everyday life had been going on for generations. The then popular critic, J. Brauner, put it this way: "The Jewish eyes have cried too often and have shed too many tears. We ought to be mature and prudent enough to approach tragic problems with the philosophical calm of the Greek Epicureans. We possess what can be called an innate sense of humour. Our tragedies, just like our mysticism, have been always balancing on the verge of the grotesque... From loftiness to being ridiculous there is but one step..."

The reality of the wartime martyrdom annihilated the seeming essentiality of such categories of thinking and, on a scale unprecedented before, petrified human destinies in a tragedy beyond which there was only silence.

There was a brief interlude in this silence, however. In the Warsaw ghetto, the world's largest Jewish concentration camp for almost half a million people, the Nazis permitted several theatres to be opened. Between December 1940, and July 1942, five such theatres functioned, three of them, Eldorado, Nowy Azazel, and Melody Palace, playing in Yiddish and two, Femina and Nowy Teatr Kameralny, in Polish. They represented all the basic genres of theatrical art, from revue (Femina) and operetta (Eldorado, Melody Palace) to dramas (Nowy Azazel, Nowy Teatr Kameralny). Their repertoires reflected in a flash, as it were, the half-century of the activity of the Jewish theatre in Poland, from Lateiner, Gordin, and Shalom Aleichem to An-Ski and Asch. There was even Molière's *L'Avare as* well as humour in the style of the prewar cabarets Morskie Oko and Qui pro Quo, transposed to and adapted in the ghetto.

The theatrical interlude in the Warsaw ghetto was only one more element of the perfidious tactic of showing victims already doomed to death a flicker of hope which would soon vanish on the way to the gas chamber.

Was this merely a caprice of the Ananke of the Jewish theatre, which revived after the catastrophe of annihilation and has existed in Poland ever since?

It certainly was not a caprice that the first soirée of Jewish songs was held at Lublin's Peretz House shortly after the liberation, attended by a group of Jewish survivors of the Nazi concentration camp in Majdanek, by Jewish partisans leaving the forest, and by Jewish-born soldiers of the First Polish Army languishing for Jewish music. Very few people today remember Diana Blumenfeld singing songs which, irrespective of the lyrics and melody, sounded to the listeners like the prayer *El Male Rahamim* (God full of compassion, a prayer for the departed recited at the funeral service) and to which they hearkened with utmost emotion.

Neither was it a caprice, but an expression of the well-understood concern to satisfy the spiritual needs of people leaving their hiding places, those coming back from various camps in the Third Reich, and those returning from exile in distant Siberia, Kazakhstan, Kirghizia, Uzbekistan, and other regions of the Soviet Union, that the Central Committee of Jews in Poland, which already functioned at that time, found ways and means to satisfy their material needs, without forgetting about their cultural needs.

Thus there was the theatre again, first in Łódź and somewhat later in Wrocław. These two towns, having the largest number of the Jewish population, alternated as the seat of the theatre. It was not until 1955 that the State Jewish Theatre, named after Esther Rachel Kamińska, found its permanent home in Warsaw.

It was not an easy task, and is not today, to outline the repertoire of the Theatre. Dissemination of Jewish culture was a relatively simple assignment, entirely natural in conditions when the mass of the Jewish people were, or could be, its exclusive, or perhaps only principal recipients. The mass means here a maximally large community of people attached to the Jewish language, employing it as a means of everyday communication between themselves, absorbing the literature created in that language. Following the extermination of Polish Jews, there remained only sad remnants of that once big. community, part of whom had ceased to speak their mother tongue or had never known it, having been brought up in an assimilated home and Polish school, in the atmosphere and the spirit of Polish culture. Those people did not know the painful irony of Shalom Aleichem's stories or the epic visions shown in Sholem Asch's novels; to them, the warm emotionality of Jewish lyrics and the moving tragedy of old Jewish legends were entirely alien.

It was only the theatre that could recall to some and bring closer to others the world of people and problems that had receded into darkness, to save from oblivion the imaginations of writers who in the past, on Polish soil, had created works in the language of the Jewish people.

Whatever has been created on this soil in the domain of spiritual culture is an integral component of Polish culture irrespective of the language in which it has been expressed, and ought to be protected and handed down to the next generations as part of the national heritage.

Thus the Jewish theatre is needed not only by the ever smaller group of people organically connected with the thousand-year-old Jewish culture, which has been changing its contents over centuries; it is also needed by the entire Polish society as an altar in a shrine where the liturgy of Polish-Jewish coexistence is taking place, born out of respect for the common past.

MUSIC

At the root of Jewish music in Poland there were two elements: religious culture and folklore.

The beginnings of Jewish religious music can be traced to biblical times, and it is difficult to say today what has survived from those times and what has accumulated throughout centuries finally to shape the style and form, melodics and colour of this music. Various influences penetrated religious music, among them songs of East and West European Jews as well as the music of the nations amongst which the Jews were living. Itinerant cantors, frequently surrounded by a small choir which provided vocal accompaniment, carried over old and new melodies of prayers and religious songs which were never free from regional influences, from folklore — not only Jewish. In the synagogue culture, the cantors' cantillations were regarded as something natural.

The individuality and musical preparation of the cantors were diversified. Some of them had seminary education and some also music education. Most of them, however, especially those from small towns, were trained by well-known *hazzanim* (cantors). Their common features were: a quick ear for music, a strong and beautiful voice, and a soulful and emotional manner of interpretation.

In the Polish territories, some of the cantors acquired legendary fame, winning popularity and recognition not only among the faithful, but also among the non-Jewish musical élite. They included the 13-year-old cantor Joel Dawid Jaszuński, called Baal-Beysyl (d. 1850), who was admired by Stanisław Moniuszko and other Polish musicians of the mid-19th century.

What contributed to the flourishing of Jewish vocal music in Poland was, above all, the construction of new synagogues in the 19th and early 20th centuries. The more magnificent the temple, the more arduous were the efforts to ensure a high vocal quality of religious services. Thanks to an improvement of the financial situation of the Jewish community and the affluence of the synagogue committees, a whole galaxy of cantors appeared in Poland, their skills matching those of the best opera singers. Many of the cantors gained worldwide renown, and numerous synagogues in West Europe and both Americas were anxious to engage them.

An important position in the field of sacral vocal culture was held by Warsaw's High Synagogue in Tłomackie Street, which functioned from 1878 until the tragic days of the Nazi occupation. During services on especially festive holidays, apart from members of the congregation, chiefly the progressive Jewish élite, only holders of special invitations were admitted to the Synagogue. Such invitations were solicited by outstanding Polish musicians and singers, clergymen, government representatives. It is worth adding that the High Synagogue in Tłomackie Street was one of the few in Poland that possessed a reformed (i.e. German) character, admitting, next to the choir, organ music accompaniment.

There were other synagogues whose cantors and choirs won world renown in the interwar period. One could mention the Nożyk synagogue in Warsaw (functioning till this day in Twarda Street), the beautiful synagogue in Warsaw's Praga district (destroyed during the war), as well as synagogues in other towns, such as Cracow, Łódź, Białystok, Lublin, Lvov, or Vilna.

The most famous of Polish cantors was Gershon Sirota (1877—1943), called "the king of cantors" and "a Jewish Caruso". He conducted services in Tłomackie Street and the Nożyk Synagogue, and, as a guest cantor, in other towns in Poland and abroad. He frequently performed in concert halls and had in his repertoire, next to religious, also secular music, including arias from well-known operas. He made numerous gramophone recordings. He was a really great dramatic tenor, with a strong but, at the same time, sweet voice, a master of coloratura. Apart from a great talent, Sirota had a thorough music education, and that was perhaps why he was at times accused of having "operatic mannerisms". His musicalness, splendid voice, and unusual abilities to improvise were regarded as "a gift of heaven". Opera companies from many countries sought to engage him, but in vain; he remained faithful to the synagogue. During the uprising in the Warsaw ghetto, he and his family were burnt in their flat at 6 Wołyńska Street.

Another outstanding cantor of the High Synagogue was, from 1925, Moshe Kusewicki (1889—1965), who alternated with Sirota. He roused ecstasy and enthusiasm. He was constantly asked to conduct services abroad, and his voice was recorded in Poland and American. When the war started he fled to the Soviet Union, where he performed as a tenor in an operatic repertoire, singing, among other places, at the Georgian Opera in Tbilisi. After the war, he settled in the United States.

Let us note some other names of prominent Polish cantors: Eliezier Gerszowich (1844—1913), David Nowakowski (1848—1923), Jakub Shmul Morogowski (1856—1943), Pinchas Minkowski (1859—1924), Moshe Abram Bernsztajn (1866—1932), Mordecai Herszman (1886—1943), Pinchas Szerman (1887—1942), Eliahu Żołądkowski (1888—1942), Boruch Schorr (1904—23). A great sensation was the brilliant cantor and composer, Josele (Josef) Rosenblat (1880—1933), an American Jew who frequently performed in Poland. His records have been bestsellers till this day.

Naturally, synagogue music was not confined merely to the activity of the cantors. The Polish synagogues were famous for their excellent choirs. Depending on the size of the synagogue, the choirs numbered several, ten-odd, or several score members. The choir of Warsaw's High Synagogue, for example, included over a hundred persons and several soloists. There were hundreds of such choirs, which were also present in secular music life. For instance, the excellent choir of the synagogue in Tłomackie Street, directed until the outbreak of the war in September 1939 by David Ajzensztadt (who was killed in the Warsaw ghetto together with his daughter, Marysia, a talented singer) frequently performed in concert halls, its repertoire comprising, next to religous music, secular works: stylized Jewish folk songs, fragments of operas and oratorios. The Ajzensztadt choir also performed before the microphones of the Polish Radio.

Bordering on folk music was Hasidic music. It was played at the courts of Hasidic zaddikim, or saintly rabbis. The Hasidic religious festivals were marked by the adoration of God, combined with singing, music, and dancing. This specific Hasidic ideology was thus characterized by one of its advocates, Nahman Braslawer (1772—1811): "Come, I'll show you a new way to God. Not through speech, but through song. We shall sing, and the heaven will understand us..."The Hasidic songs and dances were filled with ecstasy and exaltation. Their authors were mostly devout Hasidim (in Poland, their courts could be found, among other places, in Góra Kalwaria, Grójec and Warka). Some of these interesting works have been preserved till this day, either in collections or on gramphone records.

Ritual music has also been preserved, handed down from one generation to another. It added splendour to family celebrations, such as engagements, betrothals, bar mitzvahs, or funerals.

The rich Jewish folk music was for the most part the work of anonymous authors. Numerous songs have survived till today, orally transmitted to posterity. A number of collections of these songs have been published coming chiefly from the countries of Eastern Europe, in particular from the Polish territories. These are historical, love, and family songs, lullabies, as well as soldiers' songs and songs created during the Second World War, sung by partisans and the people in the ghettos. Their specific beauty and emotional contents took on a particular significance after the war.

Many interesting folk melodies have been forgotten. At the close of the 19th century, it was realized that the relics of Jewish folk music should be recorded and cultivated. Folk songs began to be collected and published. Before the war, such collections were brought out by Marek Ginzburg, Noe Pryłucki, Joel Engel, and Menachem Kipnis (1878—1942), a popular Warsaw collector and propagator of Jewish lore. He knew folklore by autopsy, as, being an orphan, he had been brought up by his eldest brother, a cantor at the Wolin synagogue. He sang during services as a choir member with such prominent cantors as Berl Miler, Jakub Shmul Morogowski, Abraham Ber Birnbaum of Częstochowa, and many others. With some of them he would go on tours of Poland, giving his own concerts of folk music and collecting folk songs. He sang for 16 years in the Choir of the Warsaw Opera and the choir of the High Synagogue in Tłomackie Street. Throughout his life, he collected Jewish ritual and folk songs and maintained lively contacts with Jewish folk singers. Among the latter he found his "nightingale", his wife Zimra Zeligfeld, who became an excellent partner of his during folk music concerts. Kipnis was also a music critic, wrote articles for the daily *Haynt*, and published in Yiddish several books on music, including *Famous Jewish Musicians, Cantors and Singers, Jewish Klezmerim in Poland,* and *From Primitive Folk Song to Symphonic Music,* as well as two collections of Jewish folk songs.

The origin of Jewish folk songs was diverse. One can discern influence from the nations amongst which the Jews were living, and thus also influences of Polish folklore. Significantly, the latter were mutual influences, as Polish folklore, too, assimilated Jewish motifs, if only those popularized by klezmer bands playing in Polish inns, at weddings, and even in manors. Quite a number of songs were created by folk poet-singers. In the 19th century, they included Welwele Zbarazher, or Beniamin Zeev Erenkrantz (1826—83), an improviser who, at the request of listeners, composed melodies and lyrics concerning current problems. He had much in common with Eliakum Kunzer (1836—1913), whose sung poetry was very versatile, ranging from a deep reflection on human fate to a description of the life of poor people and their moments of joy, from sweet, sentimental melodies to lively Hasidic dances. His poetry was a synthesis, as it were, of Slavonic and Jewish lore.

There were many more such folk artistis. The last of them was Mordecai Gebirtig (proper name: Bertig, 1877—1942), a Cracow resident, carpenter by profession, poet and songster, whose songs were taken down by fellow musicians, as he himself did not know the notes. His songs would frequently become hits sung by popular Jewish actors, such as Mali Pikon, Josele Kolodny, and by Gebirtig's daughter, Lola, and were presented on the stages of small Jewish theatres, like Azazel, Ararat, or Sambatian. In 1920, the first volume of his songs, entitled *Folksstinalekh* (In a Folk Tune) appeared, and in 1936 a collection of 50 works *Mayne lider* (My Songs) marking the 30th anniversary of his activity. On the occasion of the appearance of the latter, Menachem Kipnis wrote: "Jewish love, the Jewish family, mothers and children, Jewish poverty and privation he paints in warm, unfalsified folk colours... a specific trait of his songs is that it wrings the heart, but also warms the soul with its sweet Jewish melancholy and joyful pulsation. It is not from rich drawing-rooms, but from the bare walls of the poor little room of a Jewish craftsman that his song emanates..." Gebirtig carried on his work in the Cracow ghetto, but the songs he created there contained less sentiment and joy, and more suffering. Especially dramatic was the song *Tog fun nekume* (The Day of

Vengeance), written on 4 January 1942. He was shot and killed on 4 June 1942, while being conducted, together with other ghetto inhabitants, to the railway station to be deported to Bełżec. During the Nazi occupation, his song *S'brent, undzer Shtetl brent* (Fire, Our Town Is on Fire), written in 1938, became the hymn of the fighting ghettos and a call to fight.

Another folk artist of this kind was Israel Glatsztejn (1894—1942), whose excellent songs, such as *Klingen gleker* (Ringing Bells), won great popularity. Glatsztejn was killed in the Warsaw ghetto during the war.

Folk music was co-created by Jewish musicians called klezmerim, who first appeared in the Polish territories in the 16th century. As members of manorial or folk bands, they played in inns and at weddings, both Jewish and Polish. They were self-taught musicians who did not know the notes, but nevertheless their masterly play aroused admiration. There were also klezmerim who would become a sensation in palaces and large concert halls. One of them was Józef Michał Gusikof (1806—37), a virtuoso of *strohfiedel,* a variation on today's xylophone. His play fascinated the most outstanding musicians of the epoch, among them Karol Lipiński, Frédéric Chopin, Felix Mendelssohn-Bartholdy, Ferdinand David, Franz Liszt, and also George Sand and Lamartine. He thought himself to be a Polish Jew although he came from Szklow in Byelorussia. He played his own fantasias on Polish themes: mazurkas, polonaises, Polish, Byelorussian, and Jewish folk melodies. His performances at fairs and in Warsaw courtyards launched him on a career that was to lead him to the great concert halls of Europe, including the Paris Opera. The Polish, German, and French press of the time wrote about him extensively. Today, his name can be found in all music encyclopaedias of the world. Fascination with the sound of his strange instrument resulted in its introduction in the symphony orchestra under the name of xylophone.

Gusikof was not an exception, and neither was Jankiel from *Pan Thaddeus,* a character whose prototype was Mordko (Mordecai) Fajerman (1810—80), a cymbalist, unrivalled performer of mazurkas and polonaises, once a very popular figure in Warsaw.

The play of some of the klezmerim often served as a model for outstanding professional musicians. The talent and mastery of those folk artists were, in some way, phenomenal, and thus the magnates were eager to employ them in their palatial orchestras, where they gave concerts or played dance music. Józef Elsner, a Polish composer of the early 19th century, director of the Warsaw Opera, wrote in 1805, in a letter to the *Allgemeine Musikalische Zeitung* in Leipzig: "Jewish musicians play the polonaise in such a perfect Polish spirit that no one is likely to match them." The Czech composer František Benda, who played in a Jewish band, recalls that a blind Jew, Lebel, "played his wild dances unusually lively, in a strikingly beautiful tone, and with a brilliant, daring technique". Benda himself, and many other violinists, among them the famous Leopold Auer, recall that in their youth they learnt the proper way of holding the fiddlestick from Jewish klezmerim.

Choirs constituted the main centres of Jewish music culture in Poland. One of them was the excellent choir of the High Synagogue in Tłomackie Street, directed by a consummate musician, composer, and arranger, conductor and teacher, the author of a popular Jewish music encyclopaedia, Dawid Ajzensztadt (1890—1942), the son of a kosher butcher from Nasielsk. He started his career in the choir of the well-known cantor, Eliezer Boruchowicz of Nowy Dwór, and next sang by the side of famous cantors in Riga, Vilna, Rostov, Berlin, and from 1921 in Warsaw. The choir of the High Synagogue under his directorship added splendour not only to every religious service, but also to secular concerts. When in 1935 the Warsaw Opera was preparing the world première of *The Dybbuk* by the Italian composer (of Jewish descent), Lodovico Rocco, the author himself came to the capital and, on Saturday, went to the High Synagogue to listen to the cantor and the choir. The Ajzensztadt choir had so greatly fascinated the Italian composer that he asked the Opera's management to allow the choir sing in the prologue and epilogue of his work — and his request was promptly complied with. Ajzensztadt was also a talented composer, the author of the music to Leivick's drama *Golem*, staged at Warsaw's Polski Theatre in 1928. For some time, Ajzensztadt directed the Grosser choir of the Jewish socialist organization Bund. In the Warsaw ghetto, he was one of the conductors of the Jewish Symphony Orchestra. He was killed in Treblinka, while his 21-year-old daughter Marysia, a singer with a beautiful voice and an unusually quick ear for music, called "the nightingale of the ghetto", perished in the Warsaw ghetto.

In the interwar period, there were many excellent Jewish choirs in Poland; almost every town had one. The splendid Łódź choir Hazomir, founded by Gerszon Lewin, was directed for many years by Icchaak Zaks. That ambitious choir even succeeded in staging Verdi's opera *Traviata*. The historians of Jewish culture in Poland rightly believe that, "in the golden chain" of Jewish music culture, singing was a natural need of all.

The Jewish community took an active part in musical life in its various forms. The opera houses and concert halls were frequented by large numbers of Jews. The Jewish community, however, also attended events organized by local Jewish Music Societies, some of which, e. g. the Warsaw Society, had for some time their own orchestras. The orchestra of the Warsaw Society gave concerts, among other places, at the Nowości theatre, with the participation of well-known conductors (e. g. Kurt Pohlen from Vienna) and soloists (e. g. Imre Ungár from Budapest, a blind Jew and prizewinner at a Chopin competition). In the 1930's there was a Jewish Music Institute, Jewish music schools and courses existed as well as chamber ensembles and orchestras, both amateur and professional. Every Jewish theatre was, at the same time, a music theatre, availing itself of original works by Jewish composers, among them Icchaak Szlosberg, Dawid Bajgelman, Józef Kamiński, Izrael Szejewicz, and Henoch Kon.

A separate chapter of history is the Jews' contribution to Polish music. Many Jewish instrumentalists played in symphony orchestras. In the Warsaw Philharmonic, for example, there were: Paweł Kochański and his brother Eli, an excellent cellist and professor at the Warsaw Conservatoire Adam Furmański, Grzegorz Piatigorski, a famous cellist, trumpeter, and later also conductor, and Ludwik Urstein, a regular accompanist, called "the king of accompanists". Grzegorz Fitelberg, before he became director and first conductor, had played the second violin. Daniel Czerniawski and Izydor Lewak played the cello. After the First World War, Paweł Kochański was replaced by Mieczysław Fliederbaum, who was also a member of the excellent Warsaw Quartet, while the first violins were in the hands of, among others, Ludwik Holcman, Stanisław Dobrzyniec, Henryk Fiszman, and Szymon Englender. The place of Fitelberg was taken by Jakub Surowicz, while the second violins were entrusted to Józef Waghalter, Mieczysław Sztyglic, and Jakub Szulc, a member of the well-known Warsaw family of musicians and brother of the eminent conductor, Bronisław. Leon Szulc played the bassoon, while the viola players included Paweł Ginzburg, the father of four sons, also musicians, three of whom played in the Philharmonic orchestra. Among the violists were Henryk Szpilman, also from a well-known family of musicians, and Czesław Bem, murdered during the Nazi occupation. The pillars of the contrabass were Józef Łabuszyński and Maksymilian Halpern. The kettle-drum was in the hands of one of the country's best percussionists, Roman Szulc, from the abovementioned family, who was later won over by Sergei Koussevitzky to play in his famous Boston Symphony Orchestra. Many of those musicians were killed in the ghetto, but some, like Szymon Englender, survived, having fled to the Soviet Union.

The history of Polish music, especially in the domain of conducting, has recorded the merits of the world-renowned conductor, Grzegorz Fitelberg. His contribution to the propagation of Polish music in the world was tremendous. It was not without reason that he used to be called "the ambassador of Polish music". During every concert abroad, Fitelberg would play at least one Polish work. His greatest contribution was to the popularization of the music of the Young Poland group, of which he was a member, especially the music of the then little known Karol Szymanowski and Mieczysław Karłowicz. After the latter's tragic death in the Tatras, he completed his work *An Episode at the Masquerade,* orchestrated it, and for the first time presented to the audience. Karol Szymanowski's music won renown in concert halls throughout the world thanks to its having been included in the repertoire of such outstanding virtuosos as Artur Rubinstein and Paweł Kochański who were the composer's friends. The works of Szymanowski and other Polish composers were regularly played in world concert halls by the violinists, Bronisław Huberman, Roman Totenberg, Henryk Szeryng, Ida Haendel, and Bronisław Gimpel, the pianists, Ignacy Friedman, Maurycy Rosenthal, and Bolesław Kon, and by a host of others. The great harpsichordist, Wanda Landowska, won world fame as an excellent performer of old Polish music. The pianists of the older generation, among them Leopold Godowski, Stefan Askenaze, and Mieczysław Horszowski, never forgot during their world careers about the music of the country they came from. The pianists of the present generation, including Władysław Szpilman, Ryszard Bakst, and Tadeusz Kerner, are worthy successors of the old masters.

A significant contribution to Polish music was made by Jewish composers and composers of Jewish descent. Although their works, like the works of many an erstwhile composer, have now fallen into oblivion, they played an important role in their time.

Still popular are the works of Henryk Wieniawski (1835—80), a great virtuoso of the violin and composer. He was the son of a Lublin physician, Tobiasz Pietruszka, who had converted to Catholicism and taken the first name of Tadeusz and the surname of Wieniawski, from the Lublin suburb of Wieniawy, where he lived. Today, Henryk Wieniawski's compositions can be found in the repertoire of the greatest virtuosos and are very popular with the audience. Henryk's brother, Józef, was a less known composer, but a famous pianist.

In the second half of the 19th century, popularity was won by Adam Mincheimer (Münchheimer, 1830—1904), a composer and conductor, and — after Moniuszko's death — director of the Warsaw Opera. He was the author of four operas, among them *Otton the Archer*, with a libretto by Jan Chęciński, and *Mazepa*, based on the drama of Juliusz Słowacki. His operas were played, apart from Warsaw, in Poznań, Lvov, and Turin. He also co-authored, with Moniuszko, a ballet *Satan's Pranks*. Moreover, he wrote many works for the orchestra, suites, fantasias, solo and choral songs. He was co-founder of the Warsaw Music Society. A close friend of Moniuszko's, Mincheimer, when the author of *Halka* had died, was the chief organizer of his funeral and conducted the orchestra, which played a funeral march composed especially for the occasion. He had also organized several concerts, the receipts from which were destined for the deceased composer's family. Moreover, he revived *Halka* and prepared a new première of *The Haunted Manor*. He put in order Moniuszko's private archive, which was subsequently turned over to the Warsaw Music Society.

Another well-known composer and organizer of musical life of the time was Ludwik Grossman (1835—1915), the author of such operas as *The Fisherman from Palermo*, staged in Warsaw and Paris, and *The Voivode's Ghost*, which became a success in Warsaw, Lvov, St. Petersburg, Vienna, and Berlin. He also wrote a number of works for the orchestra and for the piano, as well as many songs. The "Grossman salon" came down in the history of Warsaw's cultural life as a place where receptions were held in honour of music celebrities visiting Warsaw and performances were given by famous artists. One could meet there eminent actors, musicians, painters, writers, among them Bolesław Prus and Henryk Sienkiewicz, as well as aristocracy and rich bourgeoisie. Grossman played host to Helena Modrzejewska (Modjeska), Peter Tchaikovsky, Anton Rubinstein, Pablo Sarasate, and many other celebrities of the epoch. In partnership with Juliusz Herman, Grossman ran a piano shop and factory trade-named Herman and Grossman. Attached to the shop was a concert hall where concerts and lectures on music subjects were given. Grossman was for some time director of the Warsaw Opera. He was also one of the founders of the Warsaw Music Society, headed by Stanisław Moniuszko.

Another popular 19th century composer was Gustaw Adolf Sonnenfeld (1837—1914), regarded as a musician of the "Vienna calibre" and called "a Polish Offenbach". He conducted bands playing light and dance music, among them the orchestra in Warsaw's Dolina Szwajcarska. He wrote — at times under the pseudonym Gustaw Adolfson — dances and fantasias. He is the author of seven operettas, including *The King of Reporters,* and *The Master's Daughter.* He collaborated with Feliks Szober, with whom he wrote a charming vaudeville *A Tour of Warsaw*, staged by Leon Schiller in 1924. He is also the author of several operas and the ballet *Melusine* and *Master Twardowski.* The latter was a tremendous success and was played for many years thereafter, attaining the number of 560 performances at the Warsaw Opera alone. When Sonnenfeld died, the Warsaw press wrote that "with the death of Adolf Sonnenfeld, a particle of 19th century Warsaw, as it were, passed away". It also said that he "died in indigence..."

Leopold Lewandowski (1831—96), a violinist, composer, and conductor, was the most outstanding author of dance music in 19th-century Poland. Called "a Polish Strauss", he wrote over 300 works, the most popular of which were his temperamental mazurkas, fiery obereks, dolorous kujawiaks, and elegant polonaises. The Polish note also resounded in his numerous cotillon waltzes, galopades, and quadrilles. He wrote more serious works as well: melodies for theatrical playes, ballets, etc., orchestral works, solo and choir songs, the most popular of the latter having been a mazurka for a male choir *Hey, Whoever Is Alive.*

Maurycy Moszkowski (1854—1925), a well-known pianist and composer of the turn of the 19th century, was the father of the so-called salon music and the author of i.a. *Spanish Dances,* popular till this day.

The 20th century can likewise boast several outstanding composers. They include Poland's first dodecaphonist, Józef Koffler (1896—1944); Karol Rathaus (1891—1954), the author of the ballets *The Last Pierrot* and *A Lion in Love* and the opera *Foreign Land;* Szymon Laks (b. 1901), who lives in Paris; and Aleksander Tansman of Łódź (b. 1898), one of the most prominent contemporary composers, the author of symphonic music, oratorios, and operas.

When speaking about the Jewish contribution to Polish music and musical culture, one should take into account not only musicians, but also musicologists and music critics. In this domain, mention is due to the musicologists: Józef W. Reiss, Zofia Lissa, and Alicja Simon, and to the critics: Maksymilian Centnerszwer, Leopold Blumental, Cezary Jellenta (Napoleon Hirszband), Menachem Kipnis, and to many others. Especially significant was the contribution of Mateusz Gliński (Hercenstein, 1892—1976), a composer, conductor, writer, and music critic, the founder and editor of the influential monthly *Muzyka*, which appeared from 1924 until the outbreak of the war. Gliński was the promoter of many music initiatives. A few years before his death, he made his famous "discovery" of correspondence allegedly addressed by Chopin to Delfina Potocka. He initiated the establishment, at the International Society for Contemporary Music, of a Polish section of which he was vice-chairman from 1924 until 1935, and the foundation of a Polish Association of Music Critics, of which he was president from 1926 until the war. When the Second World War had broken out,

Gliński, on account of his "non-Aryan" descent, was compelled to leave the country. From 1957, he resided in the United States, where he founded a Frédéric Chopin Society and an International Chopin Foundation, which he presided over until his death.

One should not overlook outstanding patrons of music. In the 19th century, they included such representatives of the Jewish plutocracy as the Kronenbergs, the Toeplitzs, Jan Bogumił Bloch, and above all Aleksander Reichman, the initiator, organizer, and executor of the project to build the Warsaw Philharmonic, which opened in 1901 and of which he was director for several years. He was also the founder, publisher, and editor of the periodical *Echo Muzyczne, Teatralne i Artystyczne.*

Jews were active not only in the field of "great music"; they also made a significant contribution to what we call show bussiness today. It is worth noting, for example, that the phonographic industry in Poland was fathered by Juliusz Feigenbaum, the founder of the Syrena Record gramophone record factory.

This diversified show business, including numerous vaudeville theatres and night clubs, needed light music. In this domain, the composers and the authors of texts were almost exclusively Jews — at least, those whose names are still known today were Jews. Among them were the precursors of jazz in Poland, the authors of fashionable dances and song hits. All these composers were unusually inventive and prolific. Most of them were at the same time conductors of their own orchestras. The most popular bands, well known from gramophone records, included those of Henryk Gold, Artur Gold, and Jerzy Petersburski, Zygmunt Karasiński and Szymon Kataszek, Fred Melodysta, Zygmunt Białostocki, and Ada Rosner. It was these orchestras that led the fashion in light music in Poland, their conductors having been precursors of new trends in popular song.

Henryk Gold was born a musician's son in 1902. His mother came from the klezmer family of the Melodystas: his father Michał, a first flute in the Warsaw Opera, died during a performance of the opera *Carmen* when Henryk was two years old. Gold learnt music from the famous Stanisław Barcewicz, and when he was 17 he became a violinist in the Warsaw Philharmonic orchestra. Later on, he founded his own band which played in Warsaw's fashionable cafés Adria, Ziemiańska, etc. He also performed before the microphones of the Polish Radio. When the Second World War broke out, he fled to the Soviet Union, where he met Jerzy Petersburski. With him he founded a mixed jazz and symphony orchestra which enjoyed great popularity. One of their concerts in Moscow was attended by 35,000 people.

Jerzy Petersburski (1897—1979), an extremely gifted composer, graduate of the conservatoires in Warsaw and Vienna, was the author of a large number of very popular songs. His famous *Tango Milonga* was to become, under the changed title *Donna Clara,* a world hit. In the United States, it was sung, for example, by the famous Al Jolson. His song *Not You, Not Me,* entitled in Fench *Amour disait folie,* was in the repertoire of Edith Piaf.

Fred Melodysta was an excellent cellist and jazz player, one of the precursors of jazz in Poland. He came from an old family of musicians. He, too, was the author of numerous song hits, but he made himself known, first of all, as an excellent arranger.

Zygmunt Białostocki was another great talent in the field of light music. His songs, beginning from the famous *Rebecca,* were sung by the whole of Poland. In terms of melodic inventiveness, he was perhaps slightly inferior to Henryk Wars (a Warsaw composer of music for many Polish films). After the war, Wars settled in America, where, as he said himself, he was hard up for a long time. Fortune smiled on him when he wrote music for a film starring a dolphin. The music became hit and appeared on gramophone records. The song of *Dolphin Flipper* was sung by such stars as Bing Crosby and Doris Day.

Albeit the fame of those musicians was transitory, they nevertheless constitute an important chapter in the history of Polish music. Their influence, though frequently short-lived, was not insignificant in their epoch. On the other hand, the great masters of serious music of world-wide renown have secured for themselves a permanent place in the history of Polish music.

PAINTING

The presence of Polish Jews in the realm of painting became noticeable relatively late, not until the middle of the 19th century. There were many reasons for this delay. The canonical prohibition contained in Moses' Pentateuch, reiterated therein several times (Ex. 20,4; Lev. 26,1; Deut. 5,8) forbade the Jews to create representational art. "Thou shalt not make thee any graven image, or any likeness of any thing that is in heaven above, or that is in the earth beneath, or that is in the waters beneath the earth", said the Lord of Israel to Moses on Mount Horeb. Obedient to this law the Jews very rarely infringed the prohibition, and the artistic imagination and talent of Jewish graphic artists could express themselves exclusively in the form of vegetable ornaments and symbols executed in wood, metal embroidery, and stone bas-reliefs. The only exception were lions and deer which we can find on ancient cult objects.

The Jewish enlightenment, *Haskalah,* was laboriously working its way across the barriers of prejudice and distrust toward the world existing outstide the insular Jewish religious community. But the external world, too, was imbued with traditional prejudices and, frequently, contempt for the Jews, a strange, closed community which spoke an incomprehensible language, wore funny, outlandish garb, cultivated "secret" customs, a community which was close and, at the same time, foreign, distant. The invisible wall that surrounded the Jewish ghettos was well guarded on both sides.

A significant feature of the presence of the first Jewish painters in Polish art was the fact that their works were thematically devoted to the legends and reality of Polish national history or to the tragic events in the struggle of a people enslaved by tsarism. This was genuinely Polish and patriotic painting.

The nestor of Polish painters of Jewish descent, Aleksander Lesser (1814—84), a native of Warsaw, studied in Warsaw, Dresden, and Munich. He painted such historical scenes as *Wincenty Kadłubek Writing the Chronicle, Skarbek Habdank, The Young Boleslaus, The Defence of Trembowla.* The greatest success was his painting *The Funeral of Five Victims Perished in 1861,* depicting a demonstration of Polish-Jewish rapprochement with the participation of Archbishop Antoni Fijałkowski, Rabbi Dov Berush Meisels, preacher Markusco Jastrow, and the prominent Jewish leader, Isaac Kramsztyk. For his portraits of Polish kings, Lesser was appointed member of Cracow's Academy of Learning.

The fate of the 1863 insurgents was depicted by the painter Aleksander Sochaczewski (1843—1923). Born at Iłowo near Łowicz, he studied at Warsaw's rabbinical school. When he was 19, he enrolled in the Warsaw School of Fine Arts. He did not complete his studies, however, because for his participation in the national demonstrations of 1861, he was sent to Siberia, where he spent over 20 years at hard labour. Having returned from exile, he settled in Vienna, where he painted many pictures portraying Siberian convicts. In 1913, on the 50th anniversary of the January Insurrection, he exhibited in Lvov 126 canvases in which he had expressed the ordeal of the Siberian exile and the suffering of the home-sick convicts. He subsequently made a gift of the paintings to the city which had extended hospitality to his exhibition.

Less dramatic were the artistic life-stories of the painters: Jan Rosen (1854—1936) and Józef (1839—1909) and Szymon (1853—1908) Buchbinder. Jan Rosen won fame as a painter of battle scenes, his best painting being *The Parade in Saski Square*. Józef Buchbinder, having studied at Warsaw's School of Fine Arts and next in Dresden, Munich, Düsseldorf, and Paris, completed his artistic education working for six years at St. Luke's Academy in Rome. He painted portraits and biblical scenes. Having returned to Poland, he was for many years artistic editor of the weekly *Tygodnik Ilustrowany*.

His brother Szymon, 14 years his junior, was, from 1879 till 1883, Jan Matejko's pupil, the second Jewish student, after Maurycy Gottlieb, to have attended the Cracow School of Fine Arts. He painted historical scenes and portraits in the style of 19th-century Dutch painting. His best works included *Sigismund III in a Goldsmith's Workshop*, *The King's Jester*, *A Young Jew in the Tallith*, and *Card Fiends*.

These few cursorily traced images of the first Polish painters of Jewish origin deserve being complemented with a more general reflection.

The talent they possessed, supported by the ideas of the Jewish enlightenment, enabled them to enter the magic circle of the fields of art hitherto closed for them. Jewish themes in principle did not appear in their works, as they did not arouse interest at that time. Art collectors to whom Jewish themes should, by the nature of things, have been emotionally close, appeared in Poland rather late. It was not a paradox that Józef Buchbinder could much more easily sell his painting of a biblical scene to a Warsaw church than his brother, Szymon, could find a buyer for his painting *A Young Jew in the Tallith*.

In the paintings of Maurycy (Mojżesz Dawid) Gottlieb (1856—79), we can find, next to elements of Polish patriotism, soulful visions of scenes described in the New Testament as well as images of prominent Jewish literary figures.

Jan Matejko called Gottlieb, after the latter's death, "a painter of great hopes", for he died when he was only 23. He left works remarkable for their thematic vastness and profundity of experience.

He was the son of a wealthy oil entrepreneur of Drohobycz. The Gottlieb family was, to a considerable extent, assimilated, as evidenced by the fact that Maurycy's father sent him to school to a Basilian monastery. Gottlieb's biographer, Mojżesz Waldman, citing the notes of the future master, wrote that no other subject save history had interested him, and thus he would spent most of the time on the dunce's bench. He was completely indifferent to ridicule on the part of his classmates, for he knew that he was the best drawer not only in his class, but also in the entire school. His teacher of drawing, Sikora, convinced his father, when Maurycy was 13, that he should take the unusually talented boy from school and do everything to make him a painter. In this way, Maurycy found himself in Michał Godlewski's school of drawing in Cracow.

In 1872, the then 16-year-old Gottlieb finished the Godlewski school and entered the Academy of Fine Arts in Vienna, where he commenced studies in the field of the then fashionable historical painting. The letters he exchanged with his sister Anna indicate that he felt more and more Polish, a feeling consolidated by the study of Polish history and his ever better command of the Polish language. In one of these letters, he wrote: "I was immensely delighted by your love for the Motherland. Do love it, so that you should not live like a slave, but like a Polish woman loving the Motherland and freedom..."

When he was in his first year at the Vienna Academy, he saw Matejko's picture *Rejtan*, exhibited at the Belvedere palace there. He would frequently come back and contemplate it for hours, trying to understand the meaning of historical painting. The picture dimmed for him the charms of the Vienna

Academy and the splendours of a student of that "school of masters", his sole desire being to work with Matejko. In 1875, he was already in his second year at the Cracow School of Fine Arts. It was in Matejko's studio that his first historical paintings were born, among them *Kościuszko Taking an Oath in Cracow, Livonian Knights Asking Sigismund Augustus for Protection against the Emperor Ferdinand, Albrecht of Brandenburg Receiving Investiture from King Sigismund the Old*, and a number of excellent portraits, including *Self Portrait in the Attire of a Nobleman*.

Gottlieb's stay in Cracow was not very long. His biographers write that one of his professors and his schoolmates forced him, through their anti-Semitic behaviour, to leave the school, even though Matejko stood up for him like his own father. He left Cracow and returned to Vienna. In his letters, however, he kept emphasizing his admiration for Matejko as a painter and man.

The awareness of the moral harm done to him in Cracow was very profound. It was perhaps that episode in his life that made him start thinking about Jewish themes, hitherto absent from his works.

In Munich, where he had moved from Vienna, he painted his major works: *Shylock and Jessica, Self-Portrait (Ahasuerus), A Jew in Arab Attire, An Old Lady Wearing a Bonnet*, and others. At that time, his artistic individuality developed and strengthened.

His trip to Rome, where he met Matejko and Siemiradzki, encouraged Gottlieb to take up in his paintings the idea of reconciliation of Poles and Jews and to show its roots on a new, more profound, ecumenical plane. He painted at this time such canvases as *Christ in Capernaum, Christ in the Synagogue*, and the dramatically expressive *Christ's Head* and *Ecce Homo*. A contemporary critic wrote: "Gottlieb's Christ is an entirely fresh figure, not by faith but by love, neither a God nor an ordinary man, but a biblical prophet, a Hebrew, speaking to the Hebrews and understandable to them."

Gottlieb's artistic output comprises a painting of particular significance, *A Jew in Prayer*. It shows Jews praying in the ancient interior of a synagogue, on a most solemn holiday devoted to prayer and fasting. The tense faces express religious passion, descent into the depths of the soul, from which a silent prayer to God emanates. In the foreground, there is a patriarchal old man and, next to him, a lad with Maurycy's features, sunk in mournful reflection. On his knees, the old man is holding the Torah, on the cover of which the young master, as though presaging his premature death, had placed an inscription in Hebrew: "Offering for the Salvation of the Soul of the late Maurycy Gottlieb".

The second generation — after Lesser, the Buchbinders, and Maurycy Gottlieb — of Jewish painters in Poland would more quickly and easily find their way to Jewish motifs and themes in their artistic work. That generation was quite numerous.

Samuel Hirszenberg (1865—1908), a native of Łódź, studied painting in Cracow and Munich. When he was only 22, he painted his first important picture, marked by an atmosphere of melancholy, so characteristic of his later works. His well-known paintings include *The Wandering Jew, Uriel Acosta, Young Spinoza*, and *A Holiday in the Ghetto*. The public at many exhibitions were greatly impressed by his monumental composition *Golus*, depicting Jews fleeing a town before pogrom on a frosty winter day, with a rabbi in front, holding the Torah in his arms. Hirszenberg was one of the first masters in the Palestinian Bezalel art school. He died a year after he went to Palestine.

Leser Ury (1861—1931) was born at Międzychód, Poznań province. He studied in Düsseldorf, Brussels, and Paris. His first paintings, chiefly genre scenes, were characterized by an academic style. Under the influence of the French impressionists, he found his own style, painted landscapes and scenes of the life of big cities, and remained faithful to this style of painting until the end. He less frequently took up biblical subjects, arriving at them already as a mature artist. Full of expression are his *The Friendship of Jonathan and David, Eleazar and Rebecca by the Well*, the triptych *Man, Adam and Eve*, and *Jeremiah*. His greatest achievements in the field of biblical painting are: *Moses*

Breaking the Tablets with Commandments and the monumental picture *The Destruction of Jeru-salem.*

Maurycy Trębacz (1861—1941), a native of Warsaw, studied in Warsaw, Cracow, and Munich. He is the author of numerous genre paintings illustrating the everyday life of the Jewish people. He was murdered by the Nazis in the Łódź ghetto when he was 80. Scenes of the Jewish life were also painted by Jakub Weinles, an excellent portraitist, and Leopold Pilichowski (1869—1933), the author of such pictures as *Betrothal* and *Listen, Israel.*

Leon Bakst (1869—1924), a native of Grodno, started with painting great compositions, but won world renown as the designer of stage sets and costumes, for such ballets as *Sheherezade, The Fire Bird,* and *Petrushka,* in which he combined the great traditions of the East with the Western traditions. Artur Markowicz (1872—1934) a native of Cracow and Wilhelm Wachtel (1875—1942) of Lvov readily took up Jewish themes, as did Zygmunt Landau (b. 1900), a native of Łódź.

Among the second generation of Polish painters of Jewish descent, mention is due to Leopold Gottlieb (1883 —1934), the younger brother of Maurycy. He studied at the Cracow Academy of Fine Arts under the guidance of Jacek Malczewski, and later in Munich and Paris. During the First World War, he volunteered for the Piłsudski legions. In that period, he painted about 200 water colours portraying prominent legionaries. He later donated the pictures to the museum at the Bezalel school in Jerusalem, where he taught shortly before his death.

It is difficult to draw a dividing line between the generation of artists born in the last decade of the 19th century and their successors born in the 20th century. Both lived and worked in a period when the word "Jew" meant deportation and death. But before this occurred, they had painted at a time of breakthrough and departure from the romantic and post-romantic philosophy of history.

At the turn of the century there appeared in Paris, which had become the capital of world art, new-comers from other countries, who found in the "Paris school" both a milieu and an atmosphere conducive to their searches. They also included Jews from Poland, the most prominent of whom were Ludwik Markus (Marcoussis) and Henryk Berlewi.

Louis Marcoussis (1883—1941), a native of Warsaw, initially studied under Józef Mehoffer at the Cracow Academy of Fine Arts, and later went to Paris. Connected at first with the impressionists, he subsequently found means of expression that suited him in cubism. His *Tour Eiffel* was a significant manifestation of the new style. In the interwar period, his name became famous the world over.

Henryk Berlewi (1894—1967) of Warsaw studied painting at the Warsaw School of Fine Arts and next in Antwerp. As early as 1913, he exhibited his first works at Warsaw's Zachęta gallery. He concerned himself with Jewish themes. After the First World War he devoted himself to so-called mechano-painting. In 1923, he was a member of the avant-garde group Blok. From 1928, he resided in Paris. He held several exhibitions in Poland and also displayed his works in Paris, London, and New York.

The life of Jecheskiel Dawid Kirschenbaum (1900—54) of Staszów was exceptionally colourful. When he was only 12, he painted signboards in his native town. He next went to Germany, where he earned a living as a caricaturist. After the 1933 events in Germany, he moved to Paris, where he attracted the attention of Georges Rouault. He worked on biblical subjects, and his prophets brought to mind the figures of saints painted by El Greco. During the war, the Germans deported his wife to a death camp in Poland, where she was murdered. His exceptionally plastic memory enabled him to recreate, after the war, the landscape of the region in which he had been brought up, the people and scenes he remembered from his childhood. His paintings from that period feature great sadness and a yearning for the Jewish world, which had been organically connected with the landscape of Polish towns and which had vanished foreever.

In independent Poland, large groupings of Jewish graphic artists existed in Warsaw, Łódź, Cracow, Vilna, and Lvov.

In 1918, a group of graphic artists and writers was formed in Łódź, taking the name Yung Yidish. The group, who published their own journal, included Jankiel Adler (1895—1949), Henoch Barciński (1896—1939), Izaak Brauner (1887—1944), Pola Lindenfeld (born 1900), and Ida Bauner (1891—1948). The main inspiration of the group came from the poet and graphic artist, Mojżesz Broderson (1890—1956). An outstanding personality among the group members was Jankiel Adler from Tuszyn near Łódź. As a young boy, he served his apprenticeship at a goldsmith's shop. When he was 17, he obtained the post of engraver of postal stamps in Serbia. Only later did he enrol in a school of artistic industry in Germany. In the 1918—20 period, he lived in Łódź, where he was active in the Yung Yidish group. In the group's journal, he published his poem I Am Singing a Prayer as well as some of his drawings. During his second stay in Germany, he became a friend of Klee. In 1933, he exhibited his works in New York. During the Second World War, he was a soldier of the Polish armed forces in the West. His first works, painted in Germany, express the striving to create an original Jewish style in art. The monumental figures which he subsequently painted were to be archetypes of Polish Jews.

In Warsaw, there was a Jewish Society for the Promotion of Fine Arts. Its activities embraced the organization of exhibitions. In 1921, a huge exhibition was opened displaying the works of, among others, Henryk Berlewi, Abraham Guterman (1899—1941), Władysław Weintraub (1891—1942), Izrael Tykociński (1855—1939), Leopold Gottlieb, Samuel Cygler (1898—1943), and Stanisława Centnerszwer (1889—1943).

A significant role in artistic life was played by Bruno Schulz. Born in Drohobycz in 1892, he studied in Vienna and Lvov. From 1924 until June 1941, he lived in Drohobycz, where he worked as a teacher of drawing in the local secondary school. It was there that he was murdered by the Nazis in 1942. He is known and valued, first of all, as a writer, the author of *Cinnamon Shops* (1934) and *The Hourglass Sanatorium* (1937). He illustrated his books himself, as he was an excellent drawer. These illustrations as well as the stories were executed in the convention of dreams and deformations.

Irrespective of the above mentioned groups representing various formal trends, Jewish graphic artists participated in the Polish national artistic life, both in Warsaw and in other large cities. For example, Jan Gotard and Eliasz Kanarek were members of the St. Lukes Fraternity, grouped around Professor Tadeusz Pruszkowski, while the brothers Efraim and Menasche Seidenbeult worked at the Warsaw School of Fine Arts.

In the two-volume *Commemorative Book* written by Józef Sandel, we find a set of biographies of Jewish graphic artists murdered by the Nazis. The list includes several score names of artists, many of whom were only beginning to mature as artists, while others had already attained full artistic maturity. In this brief outline, however, it is impossible to write even a few words about each of them, while the author lacks courage to mention only a selected few in view of the cruelty of death that made no distinction between them.

The first Jewish periodicals to apperar in Poland were Józef Perl's *Zir Ne'eman* (The Faithful Messenger, 1814) and Josef Byk's *Olath Shabat* (The Day of Sabbath, 1817—24), the organ of the Galician haskilim (representatives of the Jewish enlightenement). In 1820, the writer Szymon Kohen started publishing the journal *Bikkurei Ha-Ittim* (The Critique of Time), which was to appear for a number of years. In 1824, an annual, *Ha-Zefirah* (Dawn), appeared in Lvov, but was shortly discontinued. It was Warsaw, however, that became the main centre of the Jewish press in Poland.

The first attempt at founding a Jewish newspaper in Warsaw was the publication in 1813 of the journal *Rikzug der Franzoyzn* (The Retreat of the French), translated from Polish into Yiddish and containing reports on the Napoleonic wars. In the same year, a group of Vilna Jews asked the Tsar Alexander I for permission to publish a newspaper, but the attempt failed, since the tsarist authorities demanded a pledge that the newspaper would not publish "indecent" things (meaning, of course, disloyal things).

The strivings to publish Jewish newspapers in the Polish language began to arise in the early 19th century, which was connected with the struggle for equal rights as well as with the economic and political position of the Jews, who began to play a significant part in the country. Especially the relatively large Jewish population of Warsaw (11,911 in 1805) acutely felt the lack of their own press. This need was well understood, first of all, by the Jewish intelligentsia, although they, and especially the assimilated groups who used the Polish language in everyday life, read the Polish press, including newspapers brought out by Jewish printers and publishers, such as Nathan Glücksberg's *Gazeta Literacka* (Literary Gazette) or the women's magazine *Bronisława, czyli pamiętnik Polek* (Bronisława or the Diary of Polish Women). Jakub Szacki maintains that the most widely read *Kurier Warszawski* (Warsaw Courier) in 1823 reached a circulation of over 700 — a considerable number by contemporary standards — owing precisely to Jewish readers.

The initiative to found a journal for the Jews came from a well-known Warsaw enlightenment leader, Antoni Eisenbaum (1791—1852), a graduate of a Warsaw lycée, headmaster of the rabbinical school, the author of articles in the defence of Jews published in Polish journals. He enjoyed the support of the government circles, on which he counted in seeking to establish a newspaper for the Jews. The weekly founded and edited by Eisenbaum bore the bilingual title *Dostrzegacz Nadwiślański — Der Beobachter an der Weichsel* (Vistula Observer), its aim being "the furtherance of education among the people of Jewish religion". The weekly was printed *pagina fracta* in two languages: Polish and Yiddish. This Yiddish language of *Der Beobachter* was frequently criticized as being practically the German language printed in Hebrew type. This criticism was only in part justified, as Yiddish proper did not actually develop until the second half of the 19th century. All in all, 44 issues of the newspaper appeared: 5 in 1823 and 39 in 1824. The reason for the short life of this indisputably interesting weekly was the lack of a sufficient number of subscribers. *Der Beobachter* was a pioneer periodical that went down in the history of the Polish press as Warsaw's first Polish-Yiddish journal, edited by a Jew and published for the Jews. In spite of its deficiencies, *Der Beobachter* paved the way for the Jewish press in Poland and today constitutes a rich source of knowledge about many aspects of the life of Jews in Poland and throughout the world.

Several years later, during the November 1830 Insurrection, there began to appear a journal representing assimilatory and patriotic tendencies, entitled *Izraelita Polski* (The Polish Israelite). The life of the new journal was short: only 16 issues were brought out, printed in the State Printing Office in Warsaw. Unfortunately, all the copies of this interesting journal, important because of its engagement in the struggle for Poland's independence, were lost during the last war. One set of the copies was kept at the Library of the Przeździecki Estate, which was destroyed completely by the Nazis.

Following the suppression of the November Insurrection, there was to be no Jewish periodical for many years to come. The renewed attempts, not only in Warsaw, failed to yield the expected results. One of such attempts was made in December 1857, by Hilary (Hilel) Nussbaum, Hayyim Selig Słonimski, Jakub Rotwand, and Jakub Elsenberg, who asked the superintendent of the Warsaw School District, Mukhanov, for permission to publish a weekly *Izraelita* (Israelite), which was to be edited "in the spirit of religion and morality, adapted to the ideas of the time and the locality". The arguments supporting the need for such a journal and the enclosed detailed conspectus convinced neither the official concerned with Jewish education, Leopold Sumiński, nor the neophyte censor, Krystian Czerskier, who justified their refusal by the fact that such a journal would be harmful, as it would be conducive to the separation of the Jews from the other inhabitants.

Eventually, on the initiative of a group of Jewish intellectuals, advocates of assimilation (i. a. Henryk Toeplitz, Stanisław Kronenberg, the Natanson brothers, the Fajanses), engaged in the Polish movement for independence and with the ardent support of an outstanding Polish patriot, Rabbi Ber Meisels, a weekly *Jutrzenka — Tygodnik dla Izraelitów Polskich* (Dawn — A Weekly for Polish Israelites) was founded in Warsaw in mid-1861, It was edited by Daniel Neufeld (1814—74), a teacher by profession, the author of Judaic entries in Orgelbrand's *Great Encyclopaedia.*

The first issue of *Jutrzenka* appeared on 5 July 1861, and the last one on 23 October 1863, the total having been 121 issues. The weekly ceased to be published following the arrest and deportation to the heart of Russia of its editor, D. Neufeld, "implicated" in the affairs of the January 1863 Insurrection. In the files of the tsarist investigation commission, he was called the editor of "a Jewish revolutionary newspaper, *Jutrzenka*". Incidentally, the revolutionary character of the journal was carefully concealed for fear of interference on the part of the tsarist censorship. *Jutrzenka*, its contributors including Aleksander Kraushar, Jakub Adolf Cohn, and others, not only Jews, was superbly edited, carried rich, versatile contents, and was an expression of the deep and true patriotism of Polish Jews.

The weekly *Izraelita* (Israelite), founded three years later, which was to survive for almost half a century, was a continuation of *Jutrzenka*, that first prestigious Jewish periodical. What stimulated the foundation of the weekly was the need for "repelling the anti-Jewish campaign of slander conducted by the journal *Rola*". This publishing venture was patronized by the Jewish liberal bourgeoisie, who felt the need to have their own journal. *Izraelita* was edited by Samuel Zvi Peltyn (1831—96), a teacher of Hebrew by profession, for some time manager of the Merzbach bookshop.

The first issue of *Izraelita* appeared on 8 April 1866. The newspaper was published for 47 years, until 1912. After Peltyn's death, it was edited by Nacum Sokolow, and after him by Izrael Leon Grosglik, Jakub Adolf Cohn, Henryk Lichtenbaum, and Józef Wassercug (Wasowski). As the outstanding historian, Meir Balaban, put it, "The forty-six volumes of *Izraelita* constitute a large portion of our political history, a picture of the struggle of our fathers for human and civil rights, which precisely at that time were being taken away, thus cancelling piece by piece the equal rights granted to the Jews in Poland (1861—62) by Wielopolski, to be restored in 1905, admitting Jews to participation in Poland's political life... on the whole, a historian of culture, and also a politician, ought to study carefully this voluminous work, in order to acquaint himself from this source (perhaps not always pure) with the history of Jews in the Kingdom at the point of contact of liberalism and reaction, assimilation and Żionism". Balaban wrote that Wassercug-Wassowski "destroyed the journal both in ideological and financial terms", but his successor, Stanisław Mendelson, set it right. It is indisputable that the volumes of *Izraelita* reflect the history of the Jews in Warsaw and the Kingdom. The weekly was the first important publicist rostrum of this kind in Poland, from which the most active members of the Jewish community spoke on many, even most delicate, subjects. *Izraelita* made a great contribution in the field of Polish-Jewish rapprochement, serving Polish society as a source of information about the life of the Jews, their culture, religion, and customs. The very fact that because of its language, Izraelita had for half a century been the only widely circulated newspaper of Polish Jewry makes it an important and unique historical source.

In 1862, when *Jutrzenka* was still appearing, the eminent scholar Hayyim Selig Słonimski (1810—1909), who had arrived in Warsaw from Białystok in 1838, founded a Hebrew-language weekly *Ha-Zefirah* (Dawn). Słonimski enjoyed great esteem among the Polish intelligentsia as well as the authorities. Brought up in a religious spirit, he had a perfect command of Polish, Russian, and German, was an outstanding mathematician, physicist, astronomer, the author of scientific works published in Hebrew, such as *Mosedei Hokhmah* (Bases of Wisdom), *Kokhva de-Shavit* (Comet), *Toledot ha-Shamayim* (A History of the Skies), and many others. He was also the author of many inventions, and for example improved the computing machine invented by his father-in-law and devised a method of dispatching four telegrams over a single cable.

Defining the character of *Ha-Zefirah,* Słonimski stressed in the first issue that its chief striving would be "to put Jewish youth onto the track of knowledge and to illuminate the way for all those in need of this knowledge". *Ha-Zefirah,* though written in Hebrew, was practically the first popular-science periodical in the Polish territories. It would appear, as a daily, until 1931. Aside from the tremendous significance the journal had for the dissemination of knowledge and education, it played an outstanding role in raising the editorial standard of other Hebrew periodicals, including those which far excelled *Ha-Zefirah* in importance. On the day of the outbreak of the Second World War several score such periodicals were appearing.

The first Yiddish-language periodical in the Polish territories was the weekly *Varshoyer Yidishe Tsaytung* (1867—68), founded by Hilel Gladsztern. Only 50 issues of the weekly, which was closed down because of the lack of financial resources, were published. It nevertheless played an important part as the first Yiddish-language newspaper to be brought out in the Polish territories. Its significance consisted also in the fact that, in spite of its small circulation, but certainly a much larger number of readers, Gladsztern's weekly established a habit of reading in Yiddish and even developed a certain style of modern Jewish journalism.

The last years of the 19th century and the early 20th century were of crucial importance in the history of the Jewish press in Poland. The development of Jewish social life in various forms, the appearance of new ideological trends and thus the emergence of political parties and groupings, the ever increasing participation of representatives of Jewry in self-government and parliamentary bodies, the struggle for the "soul" of society — all this confronted the most active groups and individuals with the serious problem of reaching the masses. At that time, too, advances were made in the field of transmission techniques, printing, the organization of the press, and publicist activity. Moreover, the historical events of the turn of the century gave rise to a growing need for conscientious and matter-of-fact information, for voices of journalists and ideological leaders. In conditions of the tsarist regime, however, the establishment of new journals was difficult for the Jews, who found it easier to write for the Polish press.

In an attempt to overcome these difficulties, Jewish writers and journalists initially published so-called collections which in fact were a disguised form of journals, though brought out occasionally rather than periodically. Especially active in this field was Isaac Leib Peretz who on the occasion of holidays published so-called *Peretz-Bletlekh* (Peretz Gazettes) or *Yom Tov Bletlekh (Holiday Gazettes)*. In the period from 1862 until 1915, more than 840 such newspapers were published, 300 of them on Peretz's initiative. The contributors of these newspapers included such celebrated writers as Asch, Pinski, Kaganowski, Rajzen, Mastbojm, and many others.

Toward the close of the 19th century, on 1 January 1899, Chona Rawnicki started publishing in Cracow a fortnightly "for Jewish affairs", titled *Der Yid,* which was soon turned into a weekly. The newspaper, transferred some time later to Warsaw, appeared until 1903.

Shortly thereafter, Mordecai Spektor, one of the most active journalists in the history of the Jewish press, along with Hayyim David Hurwitz, founded a weekly *Yidishe Folkstsaytung* (The Jewish Folk Gazette). The socialist organization Bund also began to play a more active role, publishing in the last years of the 19th century *Yidisher Arbayter* (The Jewish Worker), *Arbayter Shtime* (The Voice of the Worker), and several short-lived newspapers. The more important ones, published already in the early 20th century, included *Der Veker* (Reveille, Vilna 1905), *Die Shtime fun Bund* (The Voice of the Bund, Warsaw 1909—10), and the weekly *Lebens Fragen* (Questions of Life, 1916—20), initially edited by Włodzinierz Medem.

The first Jewish bourgeois newspaper was *Der Veg* (The Road), published from 1905 till 1907. Other short-lived newspapers included *Der Telegraf* (1905—06, 164 issues) and the weekly *Fraytag* (Friday). *Unzer Lebn* (Our Life, 1907—12), published by Saul Hochberg and edited by two prominent journalists and organizers of the Jewish press, Mordecai Spektor and Zvi Pryłucki, was the prototype of a large, modern daily. Two other large Jewish dailies which survived until the last days of September 1939, were *Haynt* (Today), founded in 1908, and *Moment* established in 1910.

Until the outbreak of the First World War, there also appeared many Yiddish-language periodicals, among them such literary journals as *Roman-Tsaytung* (The Journal of Novels, 1907—08), *Teatre velt* (The World of Theatre, 1908), *Der Shtrahl* (Ray, 1910—11), *Die Yidishe Voch* (The Jewish Week, 1912—13), the Zionist *Dos Yidishe Folk* (The Jewish People, 1913—17), and many others, including humorous, religious, and specialist journals, such as *Der Hoyz Doktor* (The Family Doctor, 1912—14).

Of lesser importance in that period were Jewish newspapers and magazines published in Polish, since they had to vie with the Polish press. Some of them, such as Rudolf Okręt's *Gazeta Handlowa* (Commercial Gazette, 1864—1905), later replaced by *Nowa Gazeta* (New Gazette, 1906—18), for some time called *Ludzkość* (Humanity), a daily edited by Stanisław Kempner, were so extremely assimilatory that they could hardly be called Jewish. This could not be said of *Dziennik Polityczny, Społeczny i Literacki — Przegląd Codzienny* (Political, Social and Literary Diary — A Daily Review, 1913—14), edited by Stanisław Mendelson.

As mentioned above, the Jewish periodicals in Polish were less influential, as the Jewish intelligentsia read Polish journals, many of which were published by Jews: the Orgelbrands, the Glücksbergs, Unger, Lewental. Nonetheless, there did appear such journals as *Głos Żydowski* (The Jewish Voice) and *Życie Żydowskie* (The Jewish Life, 1906, 1917—18), both of Zionist character, whose contributors would play an important part in the Jewish press of the interwar period, to mention only Icchak Grünbaum Nacum Sokołow, Samuel Hirszhorn, Jakub Appenszlak, Natan Szwalbe, Jehoszua Gotlieb, Hersch David Nomberg, Saul Wagman, Noe Pryłucki, and many others. Stefan Lubliner and Jan Ruff published *Żagiew* (Firebrand, 1916—20), subtitled A journal of Polish youth of Jewish descent, which aimed at disseminating patriotic traditions among the Polish Jews and advanced the idea of complete Polonization of the youth of Jewish faith. Mention is also due to

Dawid Kandel's quarterly devoted to the investigation of the history of Jews in Poland (1912—13), the contributors of which included also Poles.

The regaining of independence by Poland in the autumn of 1918 released tremendous publishing initiative, not only in the Polish press, but also in the Jewish press in Yiddish, Hebrew, and Polish. It should be recalled that, according to a 1921 population census, over 2.8 million of "citizens of Mosaic faith" were living in Poland, which constituted about 10.4 per cent of the country's population. Of decisive importance for the development of the Jewish press in Poland was the large percentage of Jews among the urban population, notably in Warsaw, where 310,000 Jews were living in 1921, which made up 33 per cent of the city's population and 11 per cent of all the Jewish inhabitants of Poland, among them the politically, socially, economically, and culturally most active elements. It was these Jewish elements that immediately after the war began establishing new, or reshaping previously-existing, newspapers and magazines.

The Warsaw Jewish press, regarded as national, could boast the most efficient personnel and organizational potential, modern typographical techniques, and adequate financial resources. Its influence extended far beyond the country's frontiers, reaching numerous Jewish centres the world over.

The outbreak the First World War in 1914 disturbed the activity of the Jewish press. Most of the newspapers and magazines ceased to be published. Only two large Warsaw dailies, the aforementioned *Haynt* and *Moment,* survived the war.

The first issue of *Haynt* appeared on 22 January 1908. The daily, founded by Samuel Jakub Jackan in collaboration with the prominent Warsaw journalist, Noach Hinkelsztajn, and his brother Nechemia, a well-known Warsaw merchant, soon gained great popularity. The reasons for this included the headlining of sensational news and a diversity of interesting publicist materials. Having secured good financial foundations, the daily started publishing serious articles on political, economic, and social subjects. In independent Poland, *Haynt* became an important newspaper, representing the interests of the Jewish middle strata. In political terms, the daily stood on the ground of loyalty to the state and liberalism, and as its historians write, "while it held a progressive and democratic stance... it clung to the clearly defined Zionist-democratic and nationalist line". The management of the newspaper was in the hands of an outstanding Zionist leader, Icchak Grünbaum, which fact clearly determined the character of the newspaper. *Haynt* carried a number of interesting sections, devoted much room to the problems of industry, commerce, and culture, published novels, mostly of a sensational nature, carried a weekly page of humour, and for some time included an illustrated supplement. There was a large number of advertisements, not only by Jewish firms. In case of important events, supplements were published in the afternoon. The newspaper also had local editions. The *Alt-Nay* (Old-New) cooperative, which published *Haynt*, also brought out about 20 periodicals, including *Handels-Tsaytung* (Commercial Gazette), a weekly published from 1924, which under the changed name *Handels-Velt* (The World of Commerce) appeared until the outbreak the Second World War. For some time, this firm brought out Polish-language dailies *Nowe Słowo* (New Word, 1924, 1931—32) and *Nowy Czas* (New Time, 1929). The leading contributors of *Haynt* included Abraham Goldberg, Aaron Einhorn, David Ben-Gurion, Vladimir Zhabotynsky, Bernard Singer (Regnis), Ozjasz Thon, Josef Leszczyński, Fiszel Rottenstreich, and many others.

As Moshe Grossman writes, who during a bombardment of Warsaw on 22 September 1939, worked his way to the town hall with a two-page issue he himself had written to obtain the stamp of the censor, *Haynt* "died together with his readers... practically even before them..." The rotary presses and other typographical installations were taken by the Nazis to Germany.

Many called *Moment* the second most important Jewish daily. Where it differed from *Haynt* was not only the political profile, as it was published and edited by the folkists (populists), but also the manner of editing and the excessive space given to sensation. However, it did not lack serious articles. The daily was widely read by the Jews, its circulation exceeding 100,000 copies. It carried many advertisements, also for Polish firms. The owners of *Moment*, the first issue of which appeared on 5 November 1910, were Chaim Prużański, Eliazar Zylberberg, Magnus Kryński (the owner and headmaster of a well-known Warsaw secondary school), and Zvi Pryłucki, who, next to the excellent writer Hilel Cajtlin and the popular columnist Mośhe Justman (pen-name B. Juszzon or Ichele), was the inspiration behind the newspaper. The regular contributors included Israel Zgorodzki, Noe Pryłucki, Mark Turkow, Salomon Biber, Ben-Zion Chilinowicz, and many others. From 1924 onward, the firm publishing *Moment* also brought out an evening newspaper *Varshaver Radio*, edited by Salomon Jankowski, who developed for that newspaper a style of brief news of a sensational nature and concise articles written in a light and accessible language. The last issue of *Moment* appeared on 23 September 1939. The newspaper's building was bombed and burnt down, while the rotary presses that had survived were dismantled by the Nazis and taken away.

The orthodox press was less influential but enjoyed considerable popularity in religious circles. In 1919, on the initiative of the people grouped around the famous rabbi of Góra Kalwaria and the Agudat Israel party, a weekly *Der Yid* (The Jew) was founded, which from December 1920, appeared in Warsaw as a daily. In 1929, the newspaper was renamed *Dos Yidishe Togblat* (The Jewish Daily) and officially described as the central organ of Agudat Israel. The newspaper, which regarded itself as a "stronghold of Jewishness", was characterized by loyalty to the state. In the days preceding the outbreak of the Second World War, the leading publicist Hilel Zajdman called on the Jews for solidary struggle with the Polish people "for your freedom and ours", against barbarian Nazism. The last issue of the newspaper appeared on 31 August 1939.

Varshaver Expres was another popular non-party daily of nationwide circulation, lively and easy to read, which did not shun sensation. Founded on 25 August 1926, less than a year later it was renamed *Unzer Expres* and attained a circulation of 60,000. It published, in a concise and accessible form, many materials on political, social, economic, and international questions. Greatly popular were the "Political Chats" contributed to the newspaper by Samuel Golde. *Expres* appeared until 11 September 1939.

Many newspapers were published by Jewish workers' parties, trade unions, and left-wing youth organizations. Israel Szajn (d. 1964), in his bibliography of the Jewish press, lists several hundred titles. Below we shall discuss only the two most importants dailies: *Folkstsaytung*, the organ of the Bund organization, and *Fraind*, representing a uniform front.

After Poland had regained independence in 1918, Bund started publishing a weekly *Lebens-Fragen*, next transformed into a daily and closed down by the authorities in 1920. For several years, Bund published a considerable number of periodicals and short-lived dailies. Eventually. Bund obtained official permission to found its own journal, the weekly *Folkstsaytung*, which on 1 September 1922, was turned into a daily and became the official journal of the Bund Central Committee. It was edited collectively by leading activists of the organization, including Włodzimierz Medem, Henryk Erlich, Maurycy Orzech, Zofia Dubnow-Erlich (M. Mstisławski), Josef Chmurner (J. Leszczyński), Józef Jaszuński, and others. Frequent repressions and confiscations resulted in the newspaper's being closed down several times. Renewed licences brought about a change of the daily's name into *Unzer Folkstsaytung* and next *Naye Folkstsaytung*, The Bund organization also published a number of periodicals, among them *Forois* (Forwards, 1937—39), *Bicher-Velt* (The World of Books, 1922—29). The last issue of *Folkstsaytung* appeared on 26 September 1939.

The Communist Party of Poland, being a clandestine organization, could not legally publish any newspapers. However, the groups of Jewish communists and their sympathizers attempted to found a daily representing a uniform front. Such a newspaper actually appeared in Warsaw from 20 April 1934, until 28 March 1935. Titled *Fraind* (Friend), it was brought out by the merited publisher, Borys Kleckin. The editors included Alter Kacyzne, Symcha Lew, Kadia Mołodowska, Bernard Mark, Dawid Sfard and Zeni Elbirt. Numerous confiscations and the eventual "deciphering" by the censorship of the true character of the newspaper ended its 11-month-long existence.

Among the widely read periodicals were, e. g., *Ilustrirte Woch* (1923—28) with a large number of photos, *Unzer Velt* (1926), the monthly *Unzer Buch* (1925—26), the monthy *Globus* (1932—33), the weekly *Literatur* (1935), the progressive journal *Shrifin* (Writings, 1936—38) as well as numerous periodicals devoted to the theatre, art, education, the school, religion, and medicine, magazines for children and youth, family magazines and even matrimonial magazines. There was a large number of humorous magazines appearing in various periods, the most notable of them having been *Der Blufer* (The Bluffer, 1926—30), which did not shun sharp political, social, and moral satire.

Because of the social structure of Jewry, of substantial importance was the press dealing with questions of commerce, industry, handicrafts, and the cooperative movement. Less numerous were agricultural journals, such as *Land un Lebn* (Country and Life, 1937), the organ of the Jewish Agricultural Society. Scientific journals were also published, among them *Historishe Shrifin* (Historical Writings, 1929—33), *Yunger Historiker*, turned in time into *Bleter far Geshikhte* and edited by Rafał Mahler, Emanuel Ringelblum, and Jakub Berman, *Yedyies* (News), *Yidishe Filologie, Natur un Kultur, Der Doktor,* and many others.

According to estimates, in the last years before the outbreak of the Second World War, there appeared a total of over 200 titles, including 30 dailies, with a circulation of 790,000, including 600,000 in Yiddish, 10,000 in Hebrew, and 180,000 in Poland. This constituted about 7 per cent of all the press published in Poland.

The Hebrew-language periodicals were not read extensively. Their aim was, first of all, the cultivation of the biblical language, though not the dead one, but a developing language enriched with neologisms from modern civilization and technology.

Poland's regaining of independence created the need to establish a representative daily in the Polish language. This was important both for the Jewish readers using Polish in everyday life and because of the necessity of influencing the authorities and Polish society. One of the first dailies was founded in Cracow. Called *Nowy Dziennik* (The New Journal), it appeared until the outbreak of the Second World War, latterly under the editorship of M. Kaufer. 1919 saw the establishment in Lvov of the widely read *Chwila* (Moment) with a circulation of 35,000, the last editor of which was Henryk Heschele♪ (1939).

The most important role, however, was to be played by the Warsaw press. The first issue of *Kurier Nowy* (New Courier) appeared on 10 January 1919, but on 23 January 1920, the daily was banned because of drastic descriptions of anti-Jewish outrages. A week later, the same people started publishing a new newspaper, *Nasz Kurier* (Our Courier), edited by Szaja Lebenbaum. The daily promised well as the journal of Polish Jewry, if only because of such excellent contributors as Jakub Appenszlak, Jeremiasz Frenkel, Samuel Hirszhorn, Apolinary Hartglas, Mieczysław Centnerszwer, Stefan Karlin, Ignacy Schiper, Jakub Szacki, Daniel Rozencwajg or Saul Wagman. The life of the excellently edited *Kurier* was not an easy one. It was harassed by incessant confiscations, reflected in blank spaces. On 10 February 1923, the daily ceased to appear to be replaced several weeks later by *Nasz Przegląd* (Our Review), edited by the same group of journalists. The appearance of the daily, though bourgeois and of a Zionist character, was an important event not only in the social and cultural life of Jews in Poland, but also in the history of the Polish press. Exquisitely edited by J. Appenszlak, N. Szwalbe, S. Wagman, and D. Rozencwajg, the newspaper, because of its language, was widely read in Polish circles and frequently quoted in the Polish press as a representative Jewish journal. *Nasz Przegląd* soon gained popularity, and its circulation rose to about 50,000. The daily carried a rich news section as well as a wide variety of articles, ranging from light columns and reporting to serious political and economic reviews, but above all an extensive cultural section. It included many regular supplements, such as *Mały Przegląd* (Little Review) for young people, edited by Janusz Korczak, *Nasz Przegląd Sportowy* (Our Sports Review), *Nasz Przegląd Rozrywkowy* (Our Entertainment Review) with such sections as bridge, chess, charades, crossword puzzles, and humour, and *Nasz Przegląd Ilustrowany* (Our Illustrated Review). The last (262/8962) issue of the newspaper came out on 20 September 1939. In the years 1929—32, the publishers of *Nasz Przegląd* also brought out an evening daily *Nasz Głos Wieczorny* (Our Evening Voice), which, however, could not resist the competition of the Polish evening press. On the other hand, several Polish-language dailies, including *Dziennik Warszawski* (Warsaw Daily, 1927), and *Nowe Słowo* (New Word, 1924, 1931—32), could not withstand the competition of *Nasz Przegląd*.

Greatly popular until the outbreak of the war was the daily *5 Rano* (5 A.M.), founded on 18 March 1931, by E. Spiewak and edited by R. London. The newspaper featured mostly sensation: crime, trials, and trashy novels, while devoting little room to Jewish questions. Of a similar character was the newspaper founded by Samuel Jackan, whose intention was to create a popular daily furthering discreetly harmonious coexistence between Jews and Poles. *Ostatnie Wiadomości* (The Latest News), founded in 1929, was regarded by the more ambitious readers as a tabloid. This did not prevent *Ostatnie Wiadomości* from reaching a circulation of 150,000, an enormous figure by contemporary standards.

The Jewish periodicals published in Polish had a more difficult life, as they could hardly withstand the competition of Polish journals which were readily and widely read by Jews. A number of such periodicals did appear, however. The most noteworthy included *Opinia*, a socio-political and literary weekly representing the tendencies and thought of the Jewish intellectual élite. It began appearing on 5 February 1933, commencing its existence, despite the rampant crisis, on a solid financial basis, having a wealthy patron and publisher, the Alt-Nay cooperative, which brought out, among other things, the daily *Haynt. Opinia* was edited by Moshe Indelman, and the editorial committee included Moshe Kleinbaum, Roman Brandstaetter, and Abraham Insler. The journal, despite its élitist character, reached a relatively high circulation of 25,000. The last issue of *Opinia* (71/198) came out on 20 December 1936. Hayyim Finkelsztajn, a contributor to the weekly, puts the reasons for its being closed down thus: "Black days came also for *Opinia*, but not because financial difficulties... The authorities closed down *Opinia* because it had published a historical work by Professor Józef Klauzner on the subject of Jesus. When attempts were made to re-establish the weekly, the response came that this was impossible because Cardinal Kakowski had expressed dissatisfaction with Prof. Klauzner's publication in *Opinia*, which was closed down at his express request."

Other Polish-language periodicals also had a short life, for example *Echo Żydowskie* (Jewish Echo, 1932—34), *Lektura* (Reading, 1934), *Nasz Tygodnik* (Our Weekly, 1936), *Przekrój Tygodnia* (Weekly Review, 1935—36), *Ster* (Helm, 1937—38), *Inwalida Żydowski* (Jewish Invalid, 1922—32, Cracow), *Przegląd Społeczny* (Social Review, 1927—39, Lvov), *Nasza Jutrzenka* (Our Dawn, for youth, 1921—39), *Rolnik Żydowski* The Jewish Farmer, 1933—39). Special mention is due to the women's magazine *Ewa* (1928—33), edited by Paulina Appenszlak. Its guiding idea having been "everything about the woman and only about the woman", it enjoyed great popularity and was displayed at a press exhibition in Cologne in 1928.

Some periodicals were devoted to the history, science, art, and social life of the Jews. Worthy of note is *Miesięcznik Żydowski* (Jewish Monthly, 1930—35), edited by Zygmunt Ellenberg. The short-lived *Nowe Życie* (New Life, 1924), published by Rafał Szereszowski and edited by Professor Meir Balaban, was later replaced by the monthly *Naród* (Nation, 1928—30), *Głos Gminy Żydow-skiej* (The Voice of the Jewish Community), founded in 1937, survived until the outbreak of the Second World War.

Altogether, about 300 titles in Polish appeared in various periods between 1918 and 1939. They included 19 dailies, 153 periodicals — social, political, literary-cultural, and professional — 99 youth magazines, and as many non-periodical journals published by Jewish institutions and civic organizations. There was also a Jewish Telegraphic Agency (JTA), also known as Yidishe Telegrafen Agentur. Its founder and editor-in-chief was the well-known journalist, Mendel Mozes. The agency (1920—4 September 1939) published a bulletin in Polish, Yiddish, and English which offered a wide range of information concerning Jews and not reported by other media. The JTA had its correspondents in many cities in Poland and abroad. Its service was used by the Jewish as well as Polish press and exchanged with the Polish Telegraphic Agency and many foreign agencies. The smaller Jewish Economic Agency (Yidishe Virtshaflikhe Agentur) functioned from 1936 until 1939 and also published a bul-letin.

The outbreak of the war in 1939 put an end to the Jewish press in Poland. This vacuum was filled by the wartime press, including the legal *Gazeta Żydowska* (Jewish Gazette, 1940—42), published in Cracow and circulated throughout the General-Government, and the Łódź-based *Geto-Tsaytung*, of which 18 issues appeared in 1941. However, the lot of the Jews confined in the ghettos was faith-fully depicted by clandestine newspapers, the number of which reached 70 in the 1940—43 period.

EDUCATION

The Jews had for centuries referred to themselves as a nation of the book — Am Ha-Sefer. Not only because they possessed the Torah, a book which they believed to contain the principles and command-ments of their religion coming from God, but also because they could read and write. From early childhood, boys were taught to read and instructed to memorize the Mosaic Pentateuch and the other parts of the Hebrew Scriptures. Thus came into being and was consolidated throughout centuries one of the world's oldest systems of compulsory and universal education, which realized the principle of unity of religious instruction and upbringing.

The system of instruction was a two-grade one, but already at the basic level (*heder*) pupils could master the ability to read prayers, translate the Scriptures into Yiddish, and write in that language.

The system had survived for centuries in unaltered form and was binding on the orthodox part of the Jewish community until the last days of the Second Republic. Thus it had existed longer then the educational systems of some other nations, being something of a relic of exclusively religious instruc-tion and upbringing of young people.

The centuries-old monopoly of the religious school was the outcome of the conviction of the Jewish leaders — or, as we would say today, of the ideologists of the kahals — that the mainstay of Jewry living in the Diaspora was their complete detachment from the world of secular thought, their unconditional faithfulness to all rules of conduct laid down centuries ago, rules increasingly obsolete, formalized, and thus only devotional.

Beginning from the closing decades of the 18th century, all the fresh trends and ideologies in the Jewish community saw an important, if not the chief, objective in abolishing or at least limiting the monopoly of religious schooling. This idea guided Moses Mendelssohn and a number of other reformers grouped around him, who transferred the thought of the Jewish enlightenment — *Haskalah* — into the dim Jewish alleys in the towns and cities of the Polish Commonwealth, torn apart by the partitioning powers.

The guiding idea of the *Haskalah* was the striving for equal rights for the Jews. A means to ensure equal rights was to be emancipation from the cultural ghetto through a school which would teach in the language of the country in which the Jews were living, which could make them useful socially and professionally — thus through a secular Jewish school.

The struggle for a secular Jewish school took a different course in the various parition zones.

The following figures testify to the great interest of Jewish youth in the Prussian partition zone in the possibilities of acquiring secondary education in a secular school. In 1901 in the Prussian provinces, the following percentage of Jewish youth attended schools above primary level: 65.1 in Silesia, 60.2 in Pomerania, and 50.1 in the Poznań region, while the respective figures for Christian youth were: 4.3, 7.6, and 4.7 per cent.

The abolition of the monopoly of religious schools in the education of Jewish youth in Galicia (the Austrian partition zone) met with much greater obstacles and was accomplished several score years later than in the Prussian partition zone. This monopoly could not be broken by the enlightened Austrian monarch, Emperor Joseph II, whose decrees provided for harsh punishment for recalcitrants, nor by the fervent advocate of secular Jewish schools, Herz Homber, a disciple and friend of Mendelssohn's, who spared no effort to put the Emperor's ideas into life. The mass of the Jewish people in Galicia, living at the turn of the 18th and 19th centuries in extreme poverty, did not understand Joseph II's tolerant policy, but only knew his tax collectors who mercilessly squeezed money out of them. Nor could they free themselves from the influence of the zaddikim who performed "ministry of souls" over them and enforced blind obedience, while the soulless Galician bureaucracy were unable to pursue a more flexible educational policy toward the Jewish population whom they despised. The plan to impose secular education upon the Jews authoritatively, without awaking in them a need for breaking away from the closed circle of isolation filled with prejudice, failed as early as 1806.

The schools for Jewish boys promoted by Herz Homberg were closed down; in their stead, the kahals were permitted to open their own schools.

The first such schools were established in Tarnopol (1813) and Brody (1818). The school in Tarnopol had four grades, and instruction was conducted in German. The Brody kahal set up a commercial school with an extensive curriculum, including, as well as basic subjects, French and Italian, drawing and the science of materials. In the first three decades of the 19th century, these were the only Jewish secular schools in Galicia. Later, secular kahal schools were opened in Cracow, Lvov, and other towns.

In the second half of the last century, the situation changed radically. Whereas in 1830 only 408 Jewish children were attending primary schools in Galicia, in 1900 this number rose to over 110,000. While in 1857 there were only 556 Jewish pupils in Galician secondary schools, in 1910 there were already 6,600 Jews, or 20 per cent of all secondary school pupils.

The development of Jewish secular education also encountered serious obstacles in the Russian partition zone. In 1820, acting on the instructions of the Government Commission for Religions and

Public Education, Jakub Tugendhold opened in Warsaw three primary schools for Jewish children, located in Marszałkowska, Leszno, and Bugaj streets. A quarter of a century later, one of the private schools for Jewish girls was brought under state control. In the first decades of the 19th century, about 300 children were attending those schools, while at the close of the century this number increased to 1,000. The growth, as compared with the steep increase of the Jewish population of Warsaw, was insignificant. The reasons behind aversion to government-controlled Jewish schools were similar to those impeding the implementation in Galicia of the much earlier educational edicts of Joseph II. Secular education decreed by the authorities did not arouse the confidence of the masses, socially unawakened, enclosed for centuries within the circle of medieval religious dogmatics. The burden of supporting these schools rested on the Jewish taxpayer, although he did not regard them as Jewish schools. The aversion toward the schools increased especially in the years 1823—45, when the Hebrew language had been removed from the curriculum and replaced with geometry as applied in handicrafts.

The curriculum of Jewish primary school included: religion, Polish, German, Russian, arithmetic with geometry, calligraphy, technical drawing, and singing.

It was not until 1859 that primary schools for Jewish children were opened in Piotrków, Włocławek, Płońsk, and Kalwaria. In other towns with a large Jewish population, such as Łowicz, Kutno, Gostynin, Skierniewice, Nieszawa, Chełm, Zamość, Radom, Siedlce, or Kielce, there were no secular schools. The largest number of government-controlled Jewish schools existed in the Piotrków province, where in 1898 a total of 1,851 children were attending such schools. In 1900 in Płock, there were 127 pupils in a two-grade school for boys and 80 pupils in a similar school for girls.

How insignificent these figures were is borne out by the fact that in Warsaw at that time about 12,000 pupils were going to heders for boys and 1,200 pupils to heders for girls. If we compare these figures with corresponding data for the Prussian partition zone, it will turn out that in the latter, heder education lost its raison d'être because of the strivings for emancipation of the Jews themselves. Thus a large distance separated those two parts of the former Polish territory. The distance was one more proof that the standard and character of the culture of the Jewish community, even considering all the specific traits of that culture, was strongly dependent on many factors, among them traditional political and social restrictions towards the Jews on the part of tsarism.

The picture of the Jewish educational system in the period of partitions would be incomplete, if we overlooked rabbinical schools. There were two such schools, in Warsaw and Vilna. We shall concern ourselves only with one of them, the Warsaw rabbinical school.

The only Jewish secondary school existing in Congress Poland in 1826—63, though called a rabbinical school, was regarded by the Warsaw orthodox Jews as a secular school and combatted furiously. Aside from theological subjects (Bible, Talmud, Mishnah according to Maimonides, *Shulhan Arukh* of Joseph Qaro, moral sciences based on the Bible and Talmud, homiletics), the school's curriculum comprised Hebrew and Polish grammar, universal and Polish history, geography, mathematics, natural science as well as French, German and Russian. Polish was the chief language of instruction, and the schooling lasted five years.

The selection of the subjects indicates that the school aimed at training rabbis, preachers, and teachers for Jewish primary schools. Of the 1,200 students who had attended the school during the 37 years of its existence, very few pursued teaching careers and only one became a rabbi. He was Izaak Cylkow, who also studied philosophy at Berlin University and attended the Jewish theological seminary there. He was later a preacher at the High Synagogue in Warsaw and won fame as translator of the Old Testament into Polish.

In the Russian, and thus state-controlled, secondary schools, a quota system was in force, limiting the number of Jewish students. In the private schools, there were in principle no such restrictions, but only wealthy families could afford to send their children there. Under such circumstances, the rabbinical school greatly contributed to the shaping of the new, secular Jewish intelligentsia.

When Poland regained independence after the First World War, her population included about 3 million citizens of Judaic faith, or more than 10 per cent of the total. The reborn Polish state granted the Jews full civil rights, recognizing them as a national minority.

These guarantees were laid down in the Constitution of March 1921, which ensured to all citizens equality before the law, freedom of conscience, a right to cultivate their language, to profess freely their religion, and to establish, at their own expense, welfare and social institutions as well as schools and other educational establishments.

The realization of the constitutional rights granted to the Jews was to be based on executive acts. However, many of these regulations failed to be enacted in spite of the persistent endeavours of the Jewish parliamentary representation. This concerned, among other things, regulations in the domain of education.

In the course of, and as a result of, the First World War, the old, conservative forms of Jewish life were impaired to a considerable extent. The striving to acquire secular knowledge as a way of liberation from the cultural ghetto, formerly characteristic of the Jews living in the Prussian partition zone and a part of the Jewry in Galicia, came to be shared by the former Jewish subjects of the Russian tsar. Of great significance for these transformations were the social movements among the Jews which had crystallized earlier, but developed on a broad scale only in the reborn Poland. These movements reflected differences in philosophy between the left wing and the groups who saw the future of Polish Jewry in their participation in the construction of a Jewish national state in Palestine and in preparation for life and work in that future state.

In between these extreme ideological standpoints, which had an essential influence on the shaping of school organizations and their principles of education and curricula, represented by the Bund and the Zionists, there were intermediate groups (the two wings of Po'alei Zion, Folkspartei, the Mizrachi). Outside of the sphere of influence of these two political forces, there remained a great many orthodox Jews, politically amorphic, slavishly attached to various zaddikim, who owed their leadership of the masses to the actual or alleged merits of their predecessors rather than their personal qualifications. For the latter part of Jewry, the traditional institution of education and upbringing of youth was the heder, most often with undereducated melammedim, and the yeshiva for those capable of intricate Talmudic speculations. There was one more force exerting a strong influence on the minds of young people: the communists. The latter, however, soon relinquished the concept of education through the Jewish school, as they believed that in the capitalist state the school could not be a centre of socialist education.

A relatively large, but gradually shrinking, part of the Jewish youth, chiefly in Little Poland, attended state-controlled primary and secondary schools.

These few facts explain the situation in which the Jewish school system developed and functioned in the period 1918—39. They help us to understand the differences between Jewish schools, both as regards the language of instruction as well as the principles and purposes of education. These differences reflected the richness of the social and cultural life of the generations of Jews living in independent Poland, generations which, in spite of the growing economic impoverishment of Jewry and the intensifying anti-semitic sentiments, thus manifested various forms of struggle for the image of the young generation.

The Jewish schools were in principle privately owned, although a considerable part of them were run by voluntary organizations (societies) representing the afore-mentioned ideological principles and lines of education. The status of the private schools endowed them, after meeting various harsh requirements strictly exacted by the school authorities, some or all of the rights of state schools, but did not mean any assistance from the state or local authorities in defraying the running costs of the schools which burdened the parents and also American Jewish charitable institutions (Joint).

Only one Jewish school was under state control, namely the seminary for teachers of Judaic faith, opened in October of 1918, the first principal of which was Samuel Poznański, a preacher of the High Synagogue in Warsaw.

Instruction for children and youth was organized in the following groups of schools:

Religious schools. Schools of this type were the most numerous and had the largest number of pupils. They included the private heders, the number of which was never exactly established, since not all of them were registered by the school authorities. The number of boys attending those schools was estimated at 40,000. There were also private yeshivot.

Aside from private schools, there were establishments of religious instruction subordinated to central school boards, linked to either the ultra-conservative Agudat Israel or the more progressive, partly secular Mizrachi, Augudat Israel supervised two central boards of Horev schools for boys: in Warsaw (chairman: rabbi Abraham Mordecai Alter of Góra Kalwaria) and in Vilna (chairman: the Vilna gaon, Hayyim Ozer Grodzieński), and one central board of Beth Jacob schools for girls in Cracow (its founder was Sara Schenirer). In the mid-1930's, the afore-mentioned central boards supervised a total of 820 institutions of learning attended by 109,000 boys and girls.

In addition, there were 197 religious secondary schools (yeshivot) subordinated to the Horev central board, with a total of 19,000 students.

The Mizrachi party, a religious faction of the Zionists, had its own Yavneh central school board which supervised 220 primary schools (most frequently called Tahkemoni schools) and three secondary schools. It conducted moreover two rabbinical seminaries and four yeshivot. In the Yavneh schools, the general subjects were taught in Polish, and only in the eastern borderlands in Hebrew.

The religious schools also included communal schools financed by kahals. There were 58 such schools, including 20 in Warsaw, with a total of over 10,000 pupils.

Secular schools. As a criterion of distinction between secular and religious schools, one could adopt the role played in the curricula of those schools by religious instruction, that is, the teaching of subjects being an extension of the principles and dogmas of the Judaic faith. If the main objective of a school was the teaching of subjects most generally called secular, this was a secular school. Such a school could introduce, to a varying degree, elements of religious instruction, but they were not the main principle of education and upbringing.

In the group of secular schools, mention should be made, first of all, to the schools subordinated to the central board of Hebrew schools, Tarbut (Culture). The socio-ideological basis of those schools were the ideas, advanced by the Zionist movement already before the First World War, urging return to the Hebrew language and culture. All the subjects, save the Polish language and history, were taught in Hebrew, and the method *'ibrît ba-'ibrît* (Hebrew in Hebrew), applied already in kindergartens and first grades of the primary school, facilitated mastering Hebrew as a vernacular.

The Tarbut school system took credit for transforming the dead language of the Jewish synagogue, the language of the Holy Scriptures, prayers, and the psalter into a living language in daily use. In the Tarbut schools, the Scriptures were taught not for the purpose of religious analysis or contemplation, but chiefly as the literary substance and rich vocabulary base of the common language.

The principle adopted in those schools, of education through work, expressed a striving to detach youth from the traditional verbalism. It also reflected the ideas which had found their full expression in the Halutz movement, the romantic idea of developing the barren and desert areas of Palestine as the land of the predecessors. Return to those territories, rebuilt by the Jews themselves, was to restore to them a sense of human dignity which they had been refused during the two thousand years of the Diaspora.

The Tarbut central boards superintended 269 educational institutions, including 73 kindergartens, 183 primary schools, 9 general secondary schools, and 4 teachers' colleges. The primary schools had a total of 34,000, pupils and the secondary schools enrolled 2,700 students.

Another Jewish educational system, the Central Yiddish School Organization, known as CISzO, derived the principles of education it pursued from entirely different socio-ideological positions. CISzO was founded in 1921, in a period of great hopes for creating in Poland the conditions enabling the development of Jewish cultural autonomy under the state's patronage. Its main task was to expand and increase the number of schools offering instruction in Yiddish as the mother tongue of the Jewish masses. Its founders and supporters were the political parties of the Jewish working people: the Bund (Jewish socialist workers' party) and the left wing of the Po'alei Zion.

It was from the ideological programmes of those parties that the guidelines for the education and upbringing of youth in the CISzO schools were derived. Aside from attachment to the Yiddish language and culture and exclusion of the teaching of Hebrew (save in schools in which the parents of the pupils expressly requested Hebrew to be taught), these guidelines declared that the CISzO schools would be based on entirely modern principles of education in collectivity and through collectivity, preparing young people for independent work and life in a society free from nationalism and religious prejudice.

The CISzO schools were the only truly secular schools in Poland, not only within the Jewish educational system. Their curricula excluded religious instruction, which in the lowest grade was replaced with lectures on the origin of the world and life on the earth, and in upper grades with the science of development of societies on the basis of universal history, an element of which (not the main one) was the history of the Jews.

The pupils of the CISzO schools came chiefly from workers' and craftsmen's families, and their parents were frequently in arrears with the payment of the tuition fee. The teachers, however, thanks to their great ideological involvement at times kept on working for many weeks without receiving any remuneration. The pupils in the CISzO schools totalled about 15,000, including some 4,000 young people attending evening schools and 650 students of two secondary schools: in Vilna and Białystok.

The group of Jewish secular schools also comprised 16 institutions (kindergartens and primary schools) conducted by the Sulkult (central Jewish educational-cultural organization), with a total of over 2,300 pupils. Part of these schools offered instruction in Yiddish, while others were Yiddish-Hebrew schools, with Yiddish being the language of instruction in lower grades and Hebrew in upper grades.

Within the Jewish school system in Poland, a special role devolved to Polish-Hebrew secondary schools. There were 31 such schools, conducted as a rule by civic organizations, the most esteemed of which was the Union of Civic Associations. The selection of highly qualified teachers and the concern for good teaching results won these schools the recognition of the school authorities and the full confidence of the parents.

The picture of the Jewish educational system during the period of the Second Republic would be one-sided, if we failed to present some figures concerning Jewish pupils and students in state-controlled and non-Jewish primary and secondary schools and in institutions of higher education. In the school year 1934—35, almost 60 per cent of Jewish youth, subject to compulsory education, was attending state-controlled and municipal primary schools. In non-Jewish secondary schools, the percentage of Jews averaged 18, of which 10 per cent attended state-controlled schools.

At institutions of higher education the percentage of Jewish students tended to decline. Whereas in the 1924—25 academic year, Jews constituted 21.5 per cent of students, ten years later they made up less than 15 per cent.

THE NAZI OCCUPATION

The onslaught of Nazi Germany on Poland in September 1939, put an end to the flourishing cultural life of the Jews. From the very first days of the occupation, the Polish Jews and Poles of Jewish descent, numbering over three million, were subjected to persecutions. The Nazi doctrine and policy assumed extermination of the Jewish people. The first step was a campaign of slander against the Jews, attempting to demonstrate that the Jews in Poland had been an "element of of disintegration". The reptilian Nazi newspaper in Polish, *Nowy Kurier Warszawski*, informed its readers that numerous luminaries of the Polish scholarly and cultural life were Jews or of Jewish descent. The paper "unmasked" this "infestation with Jews" time and again, publishing the names of writers and actors whose extraction had hitherto been of no concern to anybody. It mentioned such actors as Karol Borowski, recalling that his real name was Bilauer, Tadeusz Olsza (Blomberg), Michał Znicz, Stanisław Stanisławski (Bratman), Barbara Halska (Krakauer), Zofia Terné, and Aleksander Węgierko; the film directors Stanisław Szabe (Finkelsztajn), Henryk Szaro (Szapiro), Michał Waszyński (Waks), and others. Among the writers and journalists, there were, of course, Antoni Słonimski and Julian Tuwim, as well as Anatol Stern, Jacek Frühling, Samuel Marschak, Konrad Wrzos, Michał Grydzewski (Grützhendker), the editor of *Wiadomości Literackie*, and many other names. This, however, was only the beginning (December 1939).

The situation of the Jews in the ghettos set up by the Nazis in the Polish territories has been extensively described in literature. The gehenna experienced by the ghetto inhabitants was beyond human imagination. Removed from their environment, deprived of their possessions and the possibility of practising their profession — which was especially acutely felt by the intelligentsia — the people confined to the ghettos were facing poverty and hunger. The more conscious individuals soon began to realize that the ghettos were but a stage in the process of total annihilation. Initially, ghettos, called by the Nazi administration "Jewish housing districts" (*Jüdische Wohnbezirke*), were established even in the smallest towns. Such a state of affairs did not accord with the Nazi plans for a "final solution" of the Jewish problem. Hence mass-scale resettlement and concentration of Jews in the largest ghettos followed. In effect, the Warsaw ghetto, for example, in time grew to half a million people, the density of population being 120,000 people per square kilometre, the Łódź ghetto to 200,000, and the Cracow ghetto to about 70,000, to mention only the largest ones.

The ghettos, separated by a wall from the rest of the town, began to be set up in the second half of 1940 and started to be liquidated by way of total extermination in mid-1942. Only the Łódź ghetto survived until 1944. The people confined in the ghettos included not only Polish Jews, but also citizens of other countries. In the Łódź ghetto, for example, there were about 20,000 Jews from Germany, Austria, Czechoslovakia, and Luxemburg. Aside from the Jews, many Poles whose Jewish extraction had been "proved" were forced to live in the ghettos.

Although hunger, poverty, disease, and Nazi crimes decimated the ghetto population, there nevertheless existed a specific cultural life within the ghetto walls. Especially before the extermination of the Jewish population gained full momentum, cultural workers, writers, scholars, and artists attempted to organize cultural life as a challenge to their fate. This may as well have been a form of resistance or an action designed to raise the spirits and facilitate survival in the hope of human feelings on the part of the occupying forces or an early end of the war. In the years 1940—41, nothing was being said, yet, of the crematoria of Treblinka, Majdanek, Auschwitz, and other extermination camps. At any rate, while organizing various forms of material existence, the spiritual life was not neglected. The possibilities for its continuation under these tragic conditions were considerable, as almost the whole Jewish intelligentsia had found themselves within the ghetto walls.

Initially, the development of cultural life in the ghettos seemed to be favoured by the appearances of stability and the strivings to enable at least a part of the intelligentsia to resume practising their professions. The cultural workers and artists were assisted in their endeavours by the social institutions functioning in the ghettos, such as the Jewish Social Self-Aid, the Jewish Protective Committee, or the Jewish Social Welfare Society.

The Nazis dealt a severe blow to the Jewish educational system in late November and early December 1939, when they closed down all Jewish schools. In Warsaw alone, several thousand children and youth were left out of school. The persistent endeavours of the chairman of the Judenrat, Adam Czerniakow, until the war an eminent Jewish educator, resulted in obtaining permission in mid-1940 to open primary schools and vocational courses. Similar schools and courses were also called into being in other towns, but their life was usually very short due to constant harassment by the Nazis, who ordered the closing down of one school after another "for sanitary reasons". In Łódź, the situation was somewhat better at first. When a ghetto had been established there, the Judenrat took charge of 46 schools of various types. Some of them, including secondary schools, survived until mid-1941. In the Warsaw ghetto, in its "best" initial period, there were about 20 schools conducted by various secular and religious organizations, including one for baptized children, run by Caritas.

In principle, however, clandestine instruction prevailed. Clandestine schools functioned under the auspices and with the support of the Consultative Commission of political parties. Primary schools were set up in various hospices, clubs, and canteens run by welfare institutions. The instruction was combined with social and cultural events of various kinds. Clandestine Jewish secondary schools, like Polish clandestine courses, came into being as early as the end of 1939. The instruction was organized on the same principles as "on the Aryan side". In the ghetto, the Circle of Headmasters of Jewish Schools was headed by Mateusz Frenkiel, until the war the owner and headmaster of a well-known Warsaw secondary school. As Ruta Sakowska writes in her book (*Ludzie w dzielnicy zamkniętej*, Warszawa 1975), about a thousand persons attended clandestine courses, in groups of six to ten persons, in the Warsaw ghetto. Similar forms of clandestine teaching existed in some other ghettos. In all of them, Polish was the language of instruction. For well understandable reasons, some subjects had been removed from the curricula, such as gymnastics, singing, manual work. The students of clandestine schools took examinations and received certificates which were authenticated after the war by the State Verification Commission. 172 persons received general certificates of education while in the Warsaw ghetto.

In addition, a system of vocational training was in operation in the Warsaw ghetto. The only residential school was the Nursing School at the hospital in Czyste. In mid-1941, about 2,454 persons were attending vocational courses in the Warsaw ghetto. A relatively small number of persons took part in such courses as technical, pedagogical, and medical instruction. The largest attendance (250 students in 1941) was at a course of medical instruction for combatting epidemics. Initiated by Prof. Juliusz Zwiebaum, the course could boast such outstanding lecturers as Prof. Ludwik Hirszfeld, Dr. Janusz Korczak, Dr. Mieczysław Centnerszwer, Dr. Hilary Laks as well as prominent Warsaw physicians, many of whom had found themselves in the ghetto. Lectures in the history of the Jewish health service were conducted by Prof. Meir Balaban. About 70 graduates of those courses had their certificates verified after the war, in People's Poland.

As well as didactic work, scientific research was conducted in some ghettos. Noteworthy is the activity of the historian, Dr Emanuel Ringelblum, who in mid-1940 organized a clandestine archives code-named Oneg Shabbat (The Joy of the Sabbath). Cooperating with Dr. Ringelblum was a large group of historians living in the Warsaw ghetto. The scholars collected everything, from leaflets, prints, announcements (also Nazi), official and private letters to literary and scholarly works written in the ghetto. In the face of the annihilation of the ghetto, the collection was buried in several places (allegedly three). Two sets of materials were found under the ruins of the ghetto: one in September 1946, and the other, after a long search, in December 1950. These are probably not all the materials buried, but, put in order and catologued, they constitute an extremely rich source of information about the tragic years of the Nazi occupation.

The Ringelblum archives included, as well as correspondence, accounts of personal experience, questionnaires, reports, memoirs, etc., also scientific works dealing with various aspects of the ghetto life. Some of them were the outcome of studies on political, social, and demographic problems, on the questions of food supply, culture, and health and contained rich statistical materials. These studies made possible the publication after the war of a joint work *Choroba głodowa* (Hunger Disease) as well as many other works dealing with religious life, Polish-Jewish relations, etc.

Although there were many writers, poets, and journalists within the ghetto, they did not have any opportunities to pursue their work there, except writing for such programmes as "Live Newspaper". If any works of value had been created, they were left in manuscript form. Some of them have been preserved in the Ringelblum archives. The latter include Icchak Kacenelson's (1866—1944) poem *The Day of My Great Misfortune*, published only in 1980 in Jerzy Ficowski's translation from Yiddish, of the poems of Władysław Szlengl (d. 1943), contained in the collection *Co czytałem zmarłym* (What I Was Reading to the Dead, PIW, Warszawa 1977). Other authors who actively pursued their interests in the Warsaw ghetto included Rachel Auerbach, Hilel Cajtlin, Jehoszua Gotlieb, Jehoszua Perle, Miriam Ulinower, and many others.

There was also a group of authors who wrote texts for cabarets functioning in small cafés in the Warsaw ghetto. Among them was the satirical cabaret "Live Newspaper" in the Sztuka café, directed by Władysław Szlengl in collaboration with Leonid Fikszański, a poet and satirist, Wacław Teitelbaum, and Pola Braun.

In other ghettos, such poets as Maurycy Szymel, Jerzy Kamil Weintraub, Kore (Dr. Kornreich, a Cracow lawyer and satirist), Zuzanna Ginczanka, and many others perished.

The journalists did not have much to do in the ghettos. The Polish-language *Gazeta Żydowska* (Jewish Gazette, July 1940 — August 1942), based in Cracow but distributed all over the General Governement, which also had an office in Warsaw, was published with the consent and perhaps also on the inspiration of the Nazi authorities and served in principle to transmit the decrees of the occupying forces — though not exclusively. Being officially the organ of the Judenrat, it was left a certain margin of freedom by the Nazis as regards publicist articles, information on religious, literary, historical, and artistic subjects and even reports on the everyday life, especially in the Warsaw and Cracow ghettos. For this reason, the newspaper constitutes a valuable, and, in some respects, the only source of historical information. *Gazeta Żydowska* carried reviews of theatrical performances and concerts, reports on various celebrations, and published poems, short stories, religious articles, etc. Because of the character of the newspaper, however, the Jewish journalists, with very few exceptions, refused to cooperate with it.

Another legal Jewish newspaper in Nazi-occupied Poland was the Yiddish-language *Geto Tsaytung, For Informacye, for Ordnungen un Bekantmakhungen* (Ghetto Gazette. For Information, Decrees, and Announcements). Published in Łódź, the newspaper was the official "organ of the superior of the Convent of Jewish Elders" (Chaim Rumkowski held that post). A total of 18 issues of the newspaper were published between March 17 and 21 September 1941, which, however, lacked any margin of journalistic freedom. Then there was *The Bulletin of the Ghetto Chronicle*, a hectographed periodical which appeared from 12 January 1941 until 30 July 1944 (from September 1942, in German). This important document of those years was published in book form after the war.

The Jewish press published officially during the occupation was not very widely read and certainly did not enjoy the sympathy of the inhumanly oppressed population. It was neither representative nor credible as a reflection of feelings and views, thoughts and aspirations, concerns and anxieties. It falsified the atmosphere among the masses imprisoned in the ghettos and concentration camps, who displayed an ever growing readiness for resistance and struggle.

The expectations of the ghetto population were fulfilled by the clandestine Jewish press published by various groupings: from the communists to the extreme right-wing organizations. This clandestine Jewish press, collected in part and preserved by Emanuel Ringelblum, is a unique and extremely important document of the period of the Nazi occupation. In the years 1940 to 1943, about 70 illicit periodicals appeared in the Warsaw ghetto, most of them the organs of the Bund, the communists (including the Polish Workers' Party), the Ha-Shomer ha-Za'ir, the Ha-Halutz, the Po'alei Zion and also of the assimilators (*Żagiew*).

In the initial period of organization of "Jewish dictricts", and even after they had been surrounded with walls, many inhabitants cherished the illusion of a certain stability. In spite of the extremely difficult material situation and the intensifying persecutions, a specific cultural life was developing in the ghettos, especially from mid-1940. There were two aspects of this cultural "boom". One of them was the striving to survive those tragic years. Many inhabitants of the ghettos seemed to believe in the possibility of at least a part of the population being saved, the possibility of survival thanks precisely to the enlivening of the various forms of life, including cultural life. The other reason was the presence, especially in the Warsaw ghetto, of a large number of writers, actors, musicians — Jews and Poles of Jewish descent as well as citizens of other countries of Europe. Those people sought some employment, some source of subsistence, attempting at the same time to avoid humiliating passivity. It should be added that the Central Board of the Polish Actors' Union did not extend the boycott of artistic activity during the occupation to the ghettos because of the tragic conditions of life there. The occupying forces granted, though reluctantly, permission to open theatres and organize concerts, limiting this activity, however, to works by Jewish authors or authors recognized as Jews under the Nuremberg law and prohibiting the performance of works by "Aryan" authors. The latter prohibition was cleverly circumvented, for example, by putting on the playbill the name of the translator when Molière's *L'Avare* was performed in Yiddish.

Thus, toward the close of 1940, there functioned, though under extremely difficult conditions, a number of theatres staging plays in Yiddish, such as Eldorado, Nowy Azazel, and Melody Palace, and in Polish, e. g. Femina and Nowy Teatr Kameralny. There was also a vaudeville theatre called Na Pięterku. In the summer, in practice only in 1941, performances were organized in open-air cafés, with the participation of popular actors, writers, singers, musicians, such as Michał Znicz, Stefania Grodzieńska, Jerzy Jurandot, Wiera Gran, Bolesław Norski, the "ghetto nightingale Marysia Ajzensztadt, the dancer Irena Prusicka and many musicians, including the pianist Władysław Szpilman and Leopold Rubinstein's orchestra. The revue theatres featured such stars as Franciszka Mennówna,

Diana Blumenfeld-Dybińska, Stanisław Stanisławski, Ivo Vesby, Regina Cukier, the talented actress, singer and dancer Róża Gazel, and many others. More ambitious theatres staged Jewish classics such as Asch's *God of Vengeance and* Aleichem's *The Grand Prix*, while the Nowy Teatr Kameralny, under the management of the well-known author and director Andrzej Marek (Marek Orensztejn), produced Jacob Gordin's *Mirele Efros* starring Michał Znicz, Leon Rytowski and Diana Blumenfeld, as well as Marek's *Songsters* which before the war had been staged in Poland and in other countries of Europe and im America.

The Femina music theatre specialized in light repertoire. It had its own choir and corps de ballet, including Polish dancers, and it staged operettas, some, for example *The Czardas Princess* by the Hungarian Jew Emmerich Kálmán, with updated "ghetto" libretto (a love affairs between representatives of the ghetto "high" society). Moreover special charity concerts were often organized with the participation of well-known actors, writers and musicians.

There were quite a number of musicians in the ghettos, above all in Warsaw, Łódź, and Cracow. Among the inhabitants of the Warsaw ghetto were many members of the National Philharmonic orchestra, the orchestras of the Grand Theatre, the Operetta, and the Polish Radio as well as such noted conductors as Szymon Pullman, Marian Neuteich, Adam Furmański, Ignacy Waghalter, or Izrael Hammerman. The musicians suffered extreme hardship in the ghetto. Many outstanding instrumentalists were forced to play in street bands. Some organized small chamber ensembles, to mention only the excellent string quartet, composed of Jakub Messner, Mozes Girkulski, Daniel Krakowski, and Zygmunt Bokser, or Professor Zaks's 15-member men's choir.

Thanks to the initiative of a group of music lovers and musicians and with substantial assistance from the Central Entertainment Commission of the Jewish Social Welfare Society, a Jewish Symphony Orchestra was called into being, composed of over 70 members. The orchestra was immediately confronted with great difficulties, as some groups of instruments, mainly wind instruments, were lacking and had to be replaced with others, which demanded a laborious reinstrumentation of works to be performed. Symphony Concerts were held in the hall of the Judaic Library in Tłomackie Street, in the Femina and Melody Palace theatres, as well as in the Gospoda restaurant and the orphanage of Janusz Korczak. The tickets for the concerts were inexpensive, and the poor were admitted free of charge. The receipts from some concerts were allocated for charity purposes.

The orchestra's repertoire was astoundingly rich and comprised works by Beethoven, Mozart, Tchaikovsky, Chopin, Grieg, Auber, Brahms, Haydn and, of course, the works of non-Aryan composers, such as Offenbach, Meyerbeer, Mendelssohn.

Musical activity in the Warsaw ghetto was hampered by many obstacles. First of all, the Nazis prohibited playing "Aryan" composers, which served, in a way, as a pretext for terminating musical activity. The main difficulty, however, were the now inconceivably hard conditions of existence in expectation of a terrible end. In spite of Adam Czerniakow's intercessions with the Nazi authorities, the concerts were discontinued in mid-1942. Czerniakow dreamt of developing musical life; he urged staging an opera, suggesting either Offenbach's *Les Contes d'Hoffman* or Halévy's *La Juive* or Bizet's *Carmen*. Some artistic potential, though modest, did exist, as evidenced by concerts with the participation of such soloist singers as Roman Lilian, Diana Blumenfeld, Maryla Ajzensztadt, Lena Wolfisz, Helena Ostrowska, Krystyna Golner, or Mieczysław Corti. There was a ballet company under the directorship of Renata Lachs. The concerts featured such celebrities as the pianists Bernard Berkman, Edwarda Feinstein, Krystyna Dobrzańska-Hosenbalk, Ryszard Spira, Zygmunt Wolfsohn, Władysław Szpilman, Hanna Dockelstein, Maksymilian Filar, Leon Boruński, Ryszard Werner,

Lola Strassberg, Józef Fiszhaut; the cellists Edgar Aftergut, Rafał Broches, Halina Markowicz, Henryk Reinberg, Dawid Zajdel, Ludwik Holcman, and many others.

The last chord of the music life in the Warsaw ghetto resounded at a huge meeting on 1 July 1942, convened by the chairman of the Judenrat, Adam Czerniakow, and attended by several hundred leading representatives of the Jewish community. After a shocking speech by the chairman, who presented bluntly the situation of the Jews in the ghetto, there followed a break for tea, of which Ludwik Hirszfeld thus wrote in his memoirs: "During the intermission, there resounded piano music, a selection of Chopin's preludes interspersed with tunes from 'Poland Has Not Yet Perished'. The Jews had been prohibited to play non-Jewish composers; the fact of playing Chopin at an official meeting had its significance. But I would like to inform posterity that at that last official meeting of the Judenrat, 'Poland Has Not Yet Perished' was performed. For that song, the artist, the chairman, and most of the audience could have been sent to a concentration camp. I want to assure you, however, that I did not see fear in anybody's eyes — on the contrary, the song was an expression of hope and gratitude..."

Musical life also existed, though on a smaller scale, in the ghettos of Cracow and Łódź. In Cracow, the first concert of arias and songs sung by Betta Sklutt and the tenor Henryk April was held on 22 June 1941. A dozen or so such concerts were subsequently organized, at which only "permitted" composers were played: Halévy, Meyerbeer, Mendelssohn Offenbach, Wieniawski, Anton Rubinstein, and others.

Among the musicians murdered in the Cracow ghetto were Ryszard Apte, Juliusz Hoffman, Mieczysław Hoffman, Dola Hoffman, Maria and Hanna Zimmerman, Stella Margulie, Ziuta Pflaster, and Jakub Weissman. In mid-1942, all musical activity ceased in the Cracow ghetto.

In Łódź, the musical ambitions were far greater. An orchestra was called into being, conducted by Teodor Ryder and Dawid Bajgelman. The first musical events took place in the Łódź ghetto at the beginning of 1940. There functioned the excellent choir Hazomir, directed by Dawid Bajgelman. Toward the close of 1941, about 60 musicians, singers, and actors were living in the Łódź ghetto. By mid-1942, over a hundred concerts had been given there.

The list of casualties among the Jewish musical community comprises over 200 names. A certain number of musicians confined in the ghettos were saved by their Polish colleagues and friends.

Many painters, drawers, and sculptors lived, worked, and perished in the ghettos. The outstanding painter, Mauracy Trębacz (1861—1941), died of hunger and exhaustion in the Łódź ghetto in the winter of 1941. He left shocking pictures of ghetto scenes. The excellent portraitist, Abraham Neuman (1872—1942), was killed during the liquidation of the Warsaw ghetto. Roman Kramsztyk, (1865—1942), who had come to Warsaw from Paris shortly before the war to visit his mother, was murdered in the course of deportation. His ghetto works are shocking documents of Nazi crimes. Henryk Hochman (1881—1942) the author of paintings on Jewish themes also perished. Among the victims of Nazism were, moreover, the brothers Efraim and Menashe Seidenbeutl (twins, 1903—45), Stanisława Centnerszwer (1889—1942), Józef Śliwniak, Henryk Glicensztajn (1870—1943), Adolf Behrman (1880—1943), Jan Gotard (1898—1943), Mojżesz Rynecki (1885—1942), Gela Seksztajn (1897—1944), Jakub Glasner (1897—1942). The few who survived the Nazi occupation included Jonasz Stern, Marek Oberländer, and Marek Włodarski (Henryk Streng).

Many of the artists imprisoned in the ghettos bequeathed works testifying to the martyrdom of the Jewish nation, to the determination and heroism of the people confined behind the ghetto walls and the barbed-wire fences of the concentration camps, people mercilessly condemned to death. Their drawings, water colours, and sketches are evidence of their fate and creative passion, in spite of hunger, disease, persecution, and torture. Among the authors of those documents to martyrdom were both famous and little known artists as well as amateurs. All of them attempted to commemorate in their own way the terrible years of the occupation.

The immeasurable Nazi crimes resulted not only in the extermination of over three million Polish Jews, but also in the devastation, to a considerable extent, of the centuries-old achievements of Jewish culture in Poland, a culture which is a part of Jewish culture in general and, at the same time, of culture born and developed in the Polish territories, and thus Polish culture. Fortunately, the Nazi criminals did not destroy everything. What has survived is a heritage of Jewish culture in Poland, a document to the great humanist value of that culture.

CONCLUSION

In May 1943, after the insurrection in the Warsaw ghetto had been suppressed, after the Nazis had exploded, on May 16 of that year, the High Synagogue in Tłomackie Street, the work of Leandro Marconi, to celebrate their "victory", it appeared that they had put an end to Jewish culture in Poland. But this time, too, as in their wartime strategic plans, they miscalculated. Their crimes of genocide and barbarities were unparalleled in the history of mankind. Nonetheless, they were unable to exterminate all of Polish Jewry, and the more so to destroy Jewish culture in Poland.

When the hostilities had come to an end, Polish Jews began to leave their hiding places, to return from the forests, from partisan units, from the Polish Army, from other countries. Others revealed their identity, having spent the occupation as holders of "Aryan documents" received from the Polish resistance movement or the Church.

It was those people that formed a new Jewish community after the war. Jewish cultural life was likewise revived. At present, in Warsaw and over a dozen Polish towns a Socio-Cultural Society of Jews in Poland functions. A socio-cultural weekly Folksshtime (People's Voice) is published in Yiddish and Polish. A State Jewish Theatre, named after the great actress, Esther Rachel Kamińska, exists in Warsaw.

Research work in the field of the history of Jews in Poland and the world is the concern of the Jewish Historical Institute in Poland, which has its headquarters in the reconstructed building of the Library and Institute of Judaic Sciences in Tłomackie Street (now Gen. Świerczewski Avenue). The Institute functions under the scientific and financial patronage of the Polish Academy of Sciences. Since 1950, it has been publishing a Polish-language quarterly (with summaries in English and Yiddish) entitled *Biuletyn Żydowskiego Instytutu Historycznego w Polsce* (Bulletin of the Jewish Historical Institute in Poland), of which 116 issues had appeared by the end of 1980. It has also brought out a Yiddish-language periodical *Bleter far Geshikhte* (Pages of History), of which 19 volumes (43 issues) had been published by the end of 1980. The collection of a Museum of Jewish Art, attached to the Institute, includes paintings by such famous artists as Maurycy Gottlieb, Maurycy Trębacz, Artur Markowicz, Jan Gotard, Adolf Behrman, Bruno Schulz, Jonasz Stern, and Marek Włodarski, as well as sculptures and works in metal by Abraham Ostrzega, Józef Gabowicz, Henryk Glicensztejn, Józef Śliwiak, Henryk Kuna, Alina Szapocznikow, and Romuald Gruszczyński. The Museum also boasts a rich collection of sacral art including liturgical and ritual accessories. There are three permanent exhibitions at the Institute: Gallery of Art, The Jews in Poland until 1939, and The Martyrdom and Struggle of the Jewish People during the Nazi Occupation.

The Institute's library contains over 50,000 volumes: judaica, semitica, and anti-semitica, scientific literature in all areas of the history and life of the Jews in Poland and the world. This collection — in Yiddish, Hebrew, Polish, and almost all European languages — is available to any persons interested, whether from Poland or from other countries. The library also has a rich collection of the Jewish press in various languages, several dozen Jewish encyclopaedias — likewise in various languages — as well as a unique, priceless collection of manuscripts and old prints, some of them dating from the 10th century.

There is also in Warsaw a Religious Congregation of the Judaic Faith which looks after Jewish cemeteries and synagogues and pursues religious activity.

Thus the spiritual life of the Polish Jews is continuing, an expression of this continuation being the present book.

Even if readers do not find in this book everything they would like to find, the authors ask for patience: this is not the last publication in this field. It appears, however, that what has been written here gives evidence of the richness of Jewish culture in Poland, a culture which has been saved from annihilation and continues to develop, thus contributing to the humanist heritage of mankind.

Translated by Lech Petrowicz

Torah scroll

Megillat Ester (The Scroll of Esther), parchment, Venice, 18th century

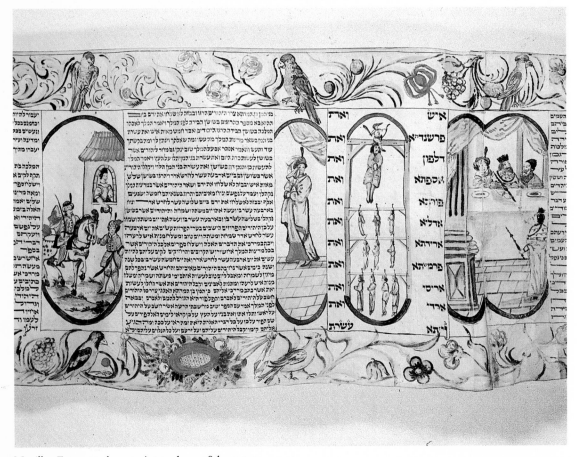

Megillat Ester, parchment, Amsterdam, 18th century

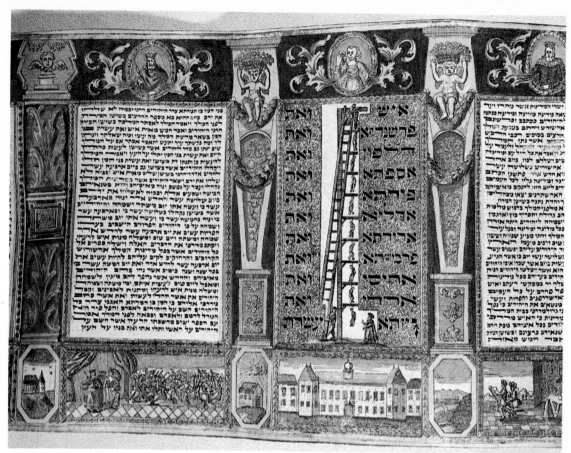

Megillat Ester, parchment, Italy, 18th century

Megillat Ester, parchment illuminated by Nathan son of Joseph,
the scribe of the Holy Books of the Torah, 18th century

Izydor Kaufman: Rabbi with a "dressed" Torah

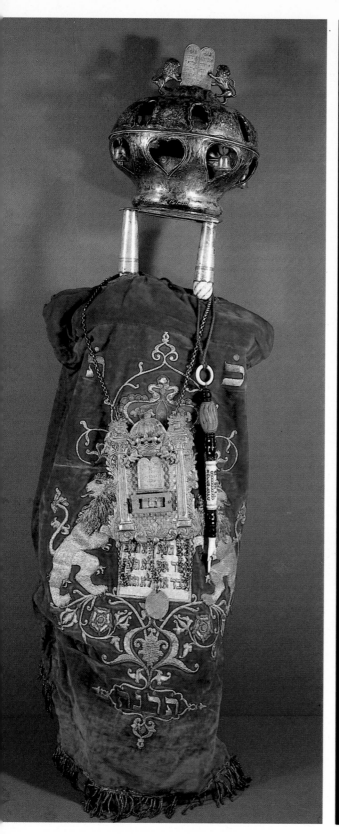

A "dressed" Torah with a crown

A "dressed" Torah with rimmonim

Torah mantle (Me'il)
with the Ten Commandments, 1896

Torah mantle (*detail*)

Parokhet, a curtain hung
before the Holy Ark (detail)

Tallit pouch, 1752

Torah crown, silver, 18th century

Torah crown, silver, 1819

Torah crown, silver, mid-19th century

Rimmonim, silver, early 20th century

Yad, a pointer used for reading the Torah, silver, 18th century

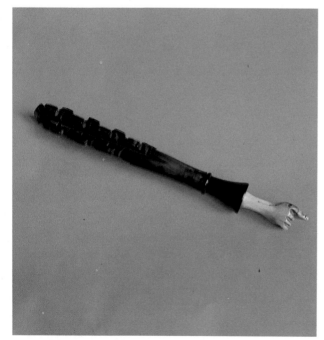

Yad, ivory and ebony, 18th century

Yad, silver, 18th century

Tas, or Torah breastplate, silver, early 18th century

Tas, silver, 18th century

Tas, silver, 18th century

Tas, gilded silver, 19th century

Tas, silver, late 19th century

Aron Kodesh, closet serving as a repository for the scrolls of the Torah, Old Synagogue in Cracow

Jakub Glazner: Interior of the Old Synagogue in Cracow

Parokhet, 18th century

116

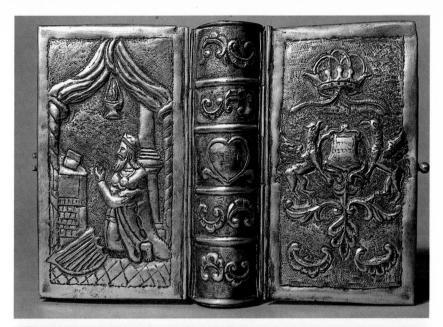

Cover of a prayer-book, silver,
18th century

Holiday yarmulka (skullcap),
18th century, and engagement ring,
19th century

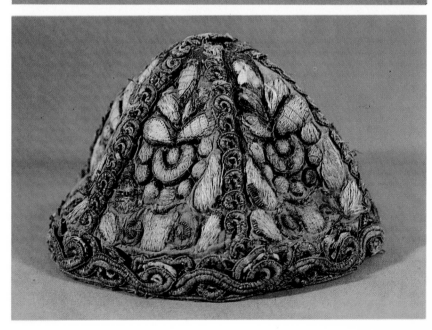

Holiday yarmulka, 18th century

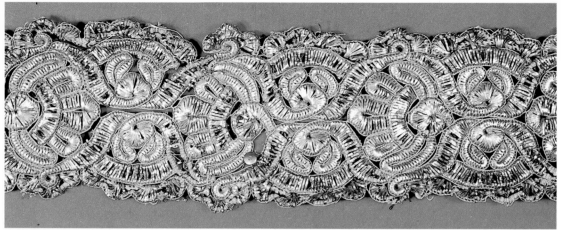

Atarah, a piece of cloth sewn with silver threads to mark the upper (i.e. the "collar") and the outer parts of the four-cornered prayer shawl

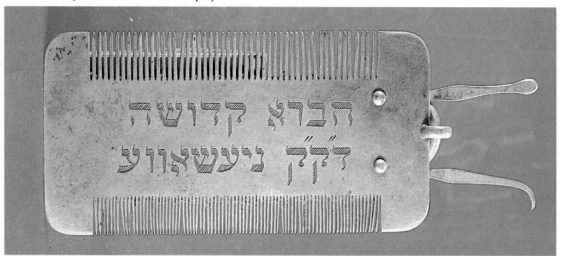

Comb of the Funeral Brotherhood in Nieszawa, silver, late 19th century

Tefillin (phylactery), a small leather case containing textes from the Pentateuch, leather, 19th century

Charity box, silver, 1901

Tefillin case, silver, 18th century

Hanukkah lamp, silver, 18th century

Hanukkah lamp, silver, 18th century

Hanukkah lamp, silver, 18th century

Hanukkah lamp, silver, 19th century

Hanukkah lamp, silver, 19th century

Hanukkah lamp, silver, 19th century

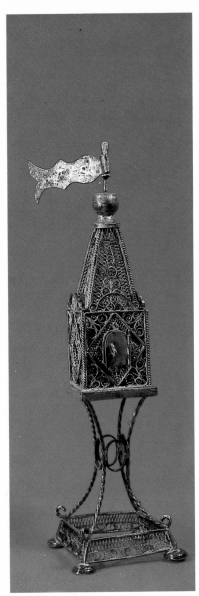

Spice box, silver,
late 18th century

Spice box, silver,
late 18th century

Spice box, silver,
2nd half of the 19th century

Spice box, silver, 2nd half of the 19th century

Spice box, silver, 2nd half of the 19th century

Box for an etrog, silver, 20th century

Box for an etrog, wood, 20th century

Sabbath plate, silver, 19th century

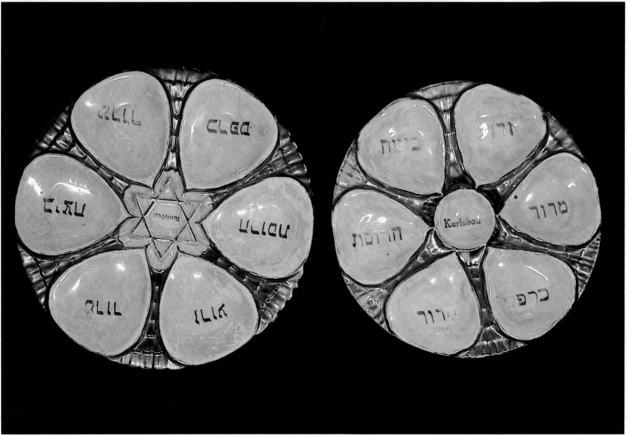

Seder plates, china, 20th century

Mazzah bag,
early 19th century

Mezuzoth, cases or tubes with a piece of parchment inscribed with passages from the Bible,
affixed to the doorpost of some Jewish homes, 20th century

Hanukkah candle-holder,
brass, 20th century

Hanukkah candle-holder,
silver, 20th century

Hanukkah candle-holder,
gilded, 19th century

Marriage certificate, parchment, Rome 1804

Nuptial canopy, 1891

Cracow. Old Synagogue, the oldest monument of Jewish sacred architecture in Poland

הכנסת חדש הרמא גדא

Cracow. Entrance to the Rema synagogue founded in the mid-16th century by the merchant Israel Isserles

Tykocin. Synagogue, 1642

134

Tykocin. Interior of the synagogue
before conservation

Details of 17th and 18th century ornaments
and Hebrew inscriptions restored
between 1974 and 1978

Zamość. Interior of the synagogue, 17th century

Rzeszów.
Old Town Synagogue,
early 17th century

Lesko. 17th century synagogue.
On the gable, quotation
from the Bible:
"How dreadful is this
but the house of God, and
this is the gate of heaven."

Dąbrowa Tarnowska. Vaulting of the synagogue decorated with polychrome representations of the signs of the Zodiac

Cracow. Tempel Synagogue, circa 1862

Tarnów. Bimah
from a synagogue burnt
down by the Nazis

Cracow. Prayer-house
of the Koba Itim
l'Torah brotherhood

143

Zygmunt Nadel: A Jew in a Fur Cap

Szymon Buchbinder: Rabbi in Prayer

Maurycy Gottlieb: Self-portrait in Eastern Costume

Maurycy Gottlieb: Ahasuerus

Maurycy Gottlieb: Portrait of Sister

Maurycy Trębacz: Portrait of an Old Man

Artur Markowicz: Prayer

Adolf Behrman: Water Carrier

Wilhelm Wachtel: Portrait of a Boy

Leopold Gottlieb: Portrait of Dr. Kupczyk

Leon Lewkowicz: Portrait of a Man with a Pipe

Józef Mittler: After a Pogrom

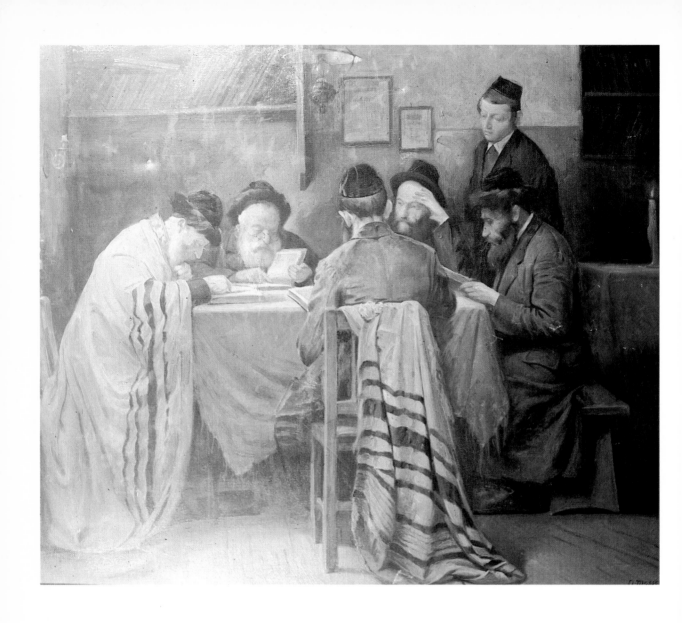

Józef Messer: Reading a Book

Rafael Lewin: The Old Synagogue in Vilna

Max Haneman: Tailor

Antoni Grabarz: Furrier

Henryk Gotlibb: Woman in a Hat

Fryc Kleiman; Jews with the Torah

Roman Kramsztyk: Portrait of a Man

Efraim and Menashe Seidenbeult: Portrait of a Man

Jan Gotard: Fairy-tale of a Cinderella

Jankiel Adler: The Last Moments of the Rabbi

Jankiel Adler: Fiddler

Jankiel Adler: My Parents

Eliasz Kanarek: Idyll

168

Marcin Kitz: A Small Town

Henryk Berlewi: Dybbuk

Adam Muszka: The Green Double-bass

Henryk Berlewi: Glazier

Bruno Schulz: Self-portrait

Roman Kramsztyk: A Jewish Family in the Ghetto

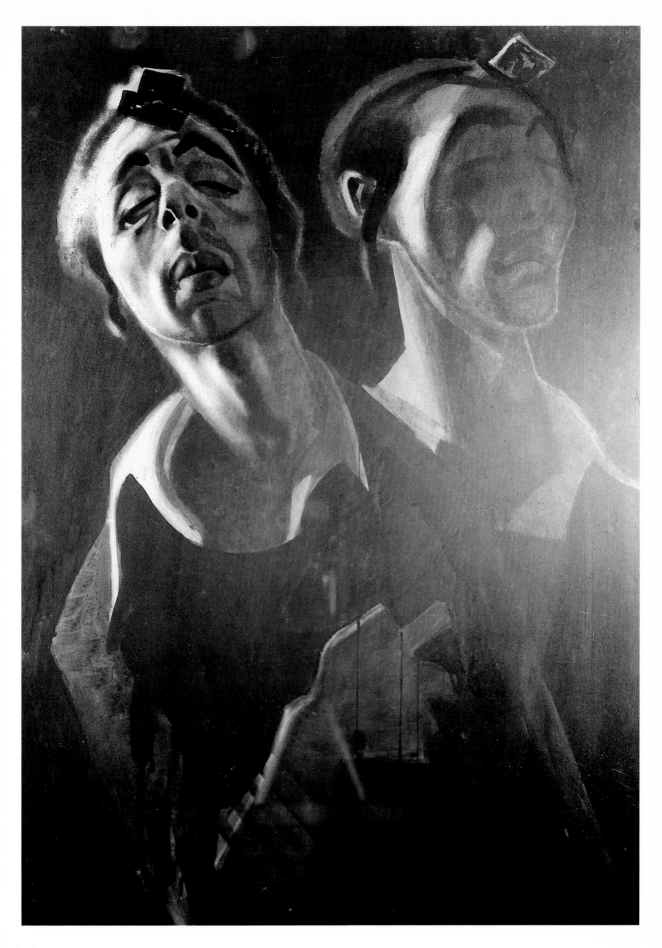

Norbert Strasberg: Ecstasy

Gela Seksztajn: Portrait of a Girl

Marek Oberländer: No More Ghettos

Cracow. Rema cemetery,
gravestone of Moses Isserles
(died 1572), prominent scholar
and Talmud commentator

Cracow. Rema cemetery, detail of the wall built after the Second World War from pieces of gravestones destroyed by the Nazis

Warsaw. Cemetery at Okopowa Street, tomb of Berek Sonnenberg (died 1826), son of the famous merchant Samuel Zbitkower

Bas-relief on the tomb of Berek Sonnenberg, with motifs referring to Psalm 137 "By the rivers of Babylon", executed by Dawid Friedlander

Warsaw. Tomb of the preacher and scholar Samuel Poznański (died 1921), designed by Henryk Stifelman

Warsaw. Tomb of Esther Rachel Kamińska (died 1925), founder of the Jewish Theatre in Warsaw.
Next to it the tomb of the actor Chewel Buzgan (died 1971)

Tomb of the writers Shalom An-ski, Jakub Beniamin Dinesohn and Isaac Leib Peretz, designed by
Abraham Ostrzega, 1924

Warsaw. Monument to the Bund members who perished during the Ghetto Uprising

Szydłowiec. Cemetery

186

Szydłowiec. Tombstone of a preacher, 1877

Ostrowiec Świętokrzyski. Cemetery

Lubaczów. Cemetery

Sieniawa. Tombstone of Jashaskel Halbersztam, 1899

Tarnów. Tombstone in the old part of the cemetery

Tarnów. 16th century tombstone

Lublin. Tomb of Jacob Isaac Hurwicz,
the "Seer of Lublin" (died 1815),
one of the founders of Hasidism

190

פה נטמן הצדקה הזאת מצבת
קודש קדושת רבינו גאון עוזנו
מאור עינינו אמרת הלבבינו וכל
בית ישראל יבכו כי חשר אור
בעריזו פן שריפת הבית אקינו
הוא יופטיר תא איש קדוש המקל
פאר התד מו כבוד הרב החסל
המפורס בכל קצבי ארומה
עקב יצחק סהרב מו אברהם
אעזר הלוי זהירוד זצוקל
אשר דכים קשיב מעוזורב
חלכו לאורו ראו שמח בנידור
שמחה הנהפר ליגון ביד פהמד
ט אבע שנת ארד עש הלבפן
תנצבה

Lesko. Cemetery

Leżajsk. Ohel (cemetery building) of zaddik Elimelech of Leżajsk (died 1787)

Chrzanów. Cemetery

Ożarów. Cemetery

Sandomierz.
Monument to the victims
of the Second World
War built
of cemetery tombstones

Sandomierz. Detail of
the monument